Y0-BGH-414

Dánca Þiarais Feiricéir

Poems, translated by Pat Muldowney

With Appendix:

The so-called Rebellion of 1641 and its Cromwellian outcome

By Brendan Clifford

AUBANE HISTORICAL SOCIETY
Aubane
Millstreet
Co. Cork

Other Aubane Publications include—

A North Cork Anthology
Bowen, Buckley, Burke, Curran, Davis, Dinneen, Eoghan Rua, etc. etc.
Edited by Jack Lane and Brendan Clifford 1993. ISBN 0 9521081 1 9

Ned Buckley's Poems
77 Poems by the Celebrated Cork Poet, With Introduction and Background Notes by
Brendan Clifford and Jack Lane 1997. ISBN 0 952108 2 7

Aubane: Notes On A Townland
A Cultural and Historical Review of the Folklore of a Corner of Co. Cork
By Jack Lane 1996. ISBN 0 9521081 3 5

250 Years Of The Butter Road — 1st. May 1748 – 1st. May 1998
By Jack Lane 1997. ISBN 0 9521081 4 3

Spotlights On Irish History — From The Confederation Of Kilkenny To The Civil War
By Brendan Clifford 1997. ISBN 0 9521081 5 1

The Cork Free Press In The Context Of The Parnell Split, The Restructuring Of Ireland
1890-1910 By Brendan Clifford 1998. ISBN 0 9521081 6 0

Aubane: Where In The World Is It?, A Microcosm Of Irish History In A Cork Townland
By Jack Lane 1999. ISBN 0 9521081 7 8

Piarais Feiriteir: Danta/Poems
With translations by Pat Muldowney
ISBN 0 9521081 8 6

is published by
Aubane Historical Society
Aubane
Millstreet
Co. Cork

© **Aubane Historical Society, 1999**

Second Edition, September 1999

This book is sold subject to the condition that it shall not,
by way of trade or otherwise, be lent, resold, hired out, or
otherwise circulated without the publisher's prior consent
in any form of binding or cover other than that in which it
is published and without a similar condition including this
condition being imposed on the subsequent purchaser.

Contents

List of Poems

3

4

I mbuan-ċuiṁne ar Tomás Ó Maoilċiaráin, 1920-1997

Tom Comber, Lahinch - Thomastown

Preface

Pierce Ferriter is the foremost of the 'Four Kerry Poets' who as a group constitute the summit of Gaelic poetical achievement. This book contains poems by him on poetry, grief, war, politics, satire, friendship, romance, erotic love, music, religious feeling, classical learning and lamentation for a destruction being wrought on a civilisation which had flourished for a thousand years. They are a unique window on that civilisation and culture. It is a great pleasure for us to continue the work of Padraig Dineen in making them available again.

There are a number of people I must thank for making this publication possible. First and foremost, Pat Muldowney, who did the translations and notes and arranged for the original poems to be presented in an attractive Gaelic script. Although, as he says himself in his introduction, it is not really possible to do full justice to Ferriter's poetry in any form of translation, I think it is possible to get a good sense of Ferriter's passions and feelings from Pat's translations. It is these feelings so well expressed that transcend the language barrier and enable Ferriter to 'talk' to us across more than three centuries. Hopefully this work will help remove the association of schooling and formal education with which he is inevitably associated in many minds.

To do as much justice as possible to Ferriter's poetry, we are producing an audio cassette of a selection of the poems, and I hope you will get a lot of pleasure from listening to them.

To put Ferriter in his historical context Brendan Clifford provides a background to the so-called Rebellion of 1641 which led to the Cromwellian terror in Ireland against which Ferriter nobly fought and by which he was ignobly murdered.

I also want to again thank IRD Duhallow for assisting us with the production costs without which this project would not be feasible.

The illustration on the cover is the ruin of Ferriter's Castle near Dun an Oir which is a poignant reminder of Ferriter and his world.

Jack Lane
Aubane Historical Society
February 1999

Introduction
Pierce Ferriter (c.1600)-1653

An article on Pierce Ferriter, written in 1969 by Art Ó Beoláin in the magazine *Comhar*, Vol. 28, concludes with a wish that Patrick Dinneen's 1934 edition of the poems be re-printed to enable more people to get to know this great poet.

Dinneen's first edition of Ferriter's poems, Dánta Piarais Feiritéir, came out in 1903. The manuscripts from which he worked were in the Royal Irish Academy. In the 1903 and 1934 editions he lists other manuscripts, in which poems by Ferriter were transcribed in the eighteenth and nineteenth centuries, held in the Franciscan Library in Killarney, the British Museum, Trinity College Dublin, University College Dublin, and St. Patrick's College Maynooth. Dinneen's 1903 edition was their first appearance in print.

Between the 1903 and 1934 editions there are some differences in the selection of poems (probably because of uncertainty regarding authorship) and in the wording of some of the poems. The 1934 edition includes a list of alternative versions of certain lines, and their manuscript sources.

The present edition includes all those poems which are definitely attributed to Ferriter by Dinneen, and, where alternative readings of some words and lines of the manuscripts exist, selects what seem likely to the editor to be the correct versions.

There is a considerable amount of additional information about Ferriter in the 1934 edition. His family was Old English; that is, Norman in origin, and they were subordinate to the Earls of Desmond (FitzGeralds). Pierce rose in the rebellion of 1641 ("rebellion" may be the wrong word; his side supported the monarch of the time), leading a body of men from Corca Dhuibhne in the Dingle peninsula to take part in the capture of Castlemaine from the English under Thomas Spring. Ferriter had previously received armaments from the English who hoped he would take their side. He then led the successful siege of the two castles in Tralee which were occupied by the English forces, and was wounded in the siege, which lasted for most of the year 1642. When Ross Castle was captured by the English in 1653 (some years after Cromwell's campaign in Ireland), Pierce went to Killarney to make terms. The terms were not agreed to, but he was promised safe conduct. On his way home he was seized at Castlemaine, brought back to Killarney, and hanged at Fair Hill (Sheep Hill) in Killarney. (Ferriter's own military conduct was more honourable; he gave the surrendering English troops in Tralee safe conduct to other English garrisons in Ireland.)

There are various poetic references to marbhadh an Dúna (*the slaughter at the Fort*, thought to be a massacre of English soldiers at the Ferriter stronghold of Dún an Óir. This was the base for the Geraldine revolt against the English and in alliance with Spain during the reign of Elizabeth I.); to ιαὸαὸ αn Ούnα (*the closing of the Castle*, when Pierce forsakes Ούn αn Όιʀ); to the injuries he received in the siege of Tralee; to incidents when he may have been a fugitive; and to the hereditary duty of the Ferriters to provide hunting hawks to the Fitzgeralds of Desmond, in return for which they held the Blasket Islands, also known as Ferriter's Islands, until the defeat of the Geraldines by Elizabeth.

The following are further sources of information about Ferriter:

State Of The County Of Kerry, Charles Smith, *1756*.

History Of Kerry, Jeremiah King.

Selections From Old Kerry Records, Series I and II, Mary Agnes Hickson.

The Journal Of The Royal Society Of Antiquaries, vol. XL.

The Keen Of The South Of Ireland, Thomas Crofton Croker, *1844*.

Journal Of The Cork Historical And Archaeological Society, vol. 5 1899.

In this edition of the poems, notes in English are given on facing pages, giving the meanings of unusual words, and unusual meanings of more familiar words. English wording for the lines is also provided. The notes and English translation have been put together with the aid of Dinneen's incomparable dictionary, and of the notes and comments in Dinneen's 1903 and 1934 editions of Ferriter. The purpose of the notes is to make Ferriter's poems accessible to readers with a basic knowledge of Irish.

It is usually possible to find English equivalents of the Irish words of the poems. But in the English notes in this edition it is merely words that are translated, not the poems themselves. The effect of the original poems derives largely from their complex metric and assonantial structure.

For instance, the first poem, *Lament For Maurice FitzGerald*, has two hundred and forty lines, in each of which the final stressed syllable is a long O sound. This is just one of the many artistic devices used by Ferriter in the poem, and they cannot be reproduced in translation. The poem is like an incantation or chant; this form of verse is called αṁʀάn or song, and it could be sung by any of the banshees or keening women mentioned near the beginning of the poem.

Other poems are in ὐάn ὐίʀεαċ (literally, *direct* (*strict, exact* or *true*) *poem*) mode, also known as bardic or syllabic; and their structure is even more complex and sophisticated. The metre of the poems is explained below in a section reproduced from Dinneen. The original spelling, and the implied pronunciation, are essential to the poems. In the (supposedly simplified) modern spelling, the poems fail to scan because of the loss of syllables which are present in the original spelling, and which should be present in correct pronunciation. In the terminology of information theory, the new spelling is a corruption or degradation of the code.

(The basic reason for the "simplified" spelling was to get around typographical problems of aspirated consonants. The solution applied by the

Grand Mikados of Free State philistinism was to eliminate those consonants, along with various associated vowel sounds. *"They never will be missed, they'll none of them be missed."* Thus, the word "séiṁiuġaḋ" (with nine letters) becomes, in English lettering, "séimhiughadh" (twelve letters), simplified to "séimhiú" (seven letters). A marginal abbreviation of spelling – from the original nine letters – was obtained. But only at the expense of, firstly, loss of consonant and vowel sounds, and secondly, making relatively simple grammatical rules (such as those for formation of the gerund[1] and participle) unnecessarily complicated. Whatever the rights and wrongs of this, modern printing enables us to use the classical, correct, simpler, more easily understood and more aesthetically pleasing version of the word just as easily as the ridiculous "simplified" version.)

The Irish language as used by Ferriter has words for many subtly different shades of meaning. (Dinneen described Ferriter's language as *"very difficult, and most interesting"*, and he occasionally gave contradictory interpretations in the 1903 and 1934 editions.) Where there are many Irish words available for something, there are sometimes few corresponding words in the English language. This again makes English translation repetitious and problematic. Ferriter describes another poet as fáiḋ foircil na ṡcóṁ-ḟocal (loosely, *"inspired master of synonyms"*) - a good description of Ferriter himself.

To illustrate the point, where English has the words *alliteration, assonance* and *rhyme*, the Irish language of Ferriter's time has the words uaim, fíoruaim, uaim cluaise, uaim ṡnúise, uaiċne, amus, aicill, coṁaroaḋ, coṁaroaḋ slán and coṁaroaḋ briste to describe various kinds of alliteration, assonance and rhyme.

In the 1903 edition Dinneen says:

> *"Ferriter's language is very difficult, and most interesting. Pressure of other work and a desire to bring out the book within a reasonable time has prevented me from giving the text the attention which it deserves. The manuscripts, too, are often unsatisfactory. There can be no doubt that Ferriter was very learned in Irish, and had a unique command of that language for poetical purposes."*

The notes in English should be used, where necessary and where possible, as an aid to negotiating the poems of Ferriter in their original form. This still leaves a considerable amount to the intelligence of the reader. Even in modern Irish, a word-for-word translation into English does not capture the meaning of many current Irish phrases. For instance, scaoil ċun siúil (literally, *release to walk*) means discharge, sack or dismiss; staiṡre beo (literally, *living (=moving) staircase*) means escalator. Nearly four centuries

---

[1]Gerund is the verbal noun, formed by adding aḋ to the verb root in the old spelling.

9

have passed since Ferriter composed these poems, and the metaphors, allusions and language are often unclear. So the English notes should be used with caution.

The Irish alphabet consists of the following letters:

ᴀ b c ᴅ e ꝼ ᵹ h ı l m n o p ʀ ꞅ ꞇ u, corresponding to

a b c d e f g h i l m n o p r s t u.

(ʀ and ꞅ also have the older representations ꞃ and ꞅ, respectively.)

There are ten basic vowel sounds in Irish, corresponding to long and short forms of ᴀ, e, ı, o, u (for example, ᴀ short, ᴀ́ long), in addition to thirteen diphthongs and five triphthongs.

Most of the consonants have so-called broad and slender forms, depending on whether the succeeding or preceding vowel in the word is broad (ᴀ, o, u) or slender (e, ı). In addition to these basic consonants, there are aspirated and eclipsed forms of many of the consonants; e.g. b has aspirated form ḃ (often written bh), and eclipsed form mb. Aspiration of a consonant makes it softer, guttural or silent, depending on the consonant. Eclipsing produces a sound similar to the eclipsing consonant. The consonants l, n and ʀ also have ll, nn and ʀʀ forms, which, unlike English, have subtly different pronunciations.

The total number of vowel and consonant sounds in Irish is therefore very large, and Ferriter made powerful use of them in his poetry.

Much of the energy and feeling of the poems results from their sound, including their metric, rhythmic, assonantial and alliterative structure. This can only be experienced by reading or listening to the Irish originals, and the accompanying notes in English are intended to assist the reader in this.

Dinneen's analysis of the structure of the poems, reproduced below from his 1903 edition, is a valuable guide. The Poem numbers in roman numerals refer to Dinneen's 1903 edition, and the arabic numbers in square brackets refer to the numbering in this edition.

Pat Muldowney, January 1999.

The Metre

The principal poems of Pierce Ferriter are written in the Elegiac Metre, although he has also used extensively the ᴅᴀ́n ᴅíʀeᴀċ.

The Elegiac Metre is used principally for the Cᴀoıneᴀḋ or Mᴀʀḃnᴀ, but not confined to that species of composition; thus Poem II [2] is in Elegiac Metre, though not a Cᴀoıneᴀḋ. The Cᴀoıneᴀḋ, as well as the majority of poems in the Elegiac Metre, is divided into stanzas of four lines each. Each line is generally ruled by four stresses on four root vowels of the line. Of these four the second and third stressed vowels correspond in sound. The first stressed vowel does not necessarily correspond in sound with any other either in that line or in any other. The final stressed vowels of all the lines in the stanza and in the entire poem correspond in sound. Correspondence of vowels means that, if simple vowels they are absolutely the same; if diphthongs or triphthongs the main sounds of the combinations are identical. Thus the vowels céiR, ɑol, ɑeR, Lɑe, bé. correspond in vowel sounds. We have stated the general rules for the Elegiac Metre, but some stanzas of Ferriter's Cɑoıneɑö are differently set. In these he employs only three stresses, the first and second falling on corresponding vowels. We give in illustration the first stanza of his Cɑoıneɑö on Maurice FitzGerald:-

> ꝉno ċRɑoċɑö ıs mo śɑoċ Rem Ló ċú,
> ꓮ ĊıɑRRɑıöıȝ ıꝺ ċıɑn-Luıȝe ı ȝcoꝼꝺRɑınn,
> ꝉno ċReɑċ c'ꝼeɑRc cɑR LeɑR ı öꝼLónꝺRɑs,
> ꓮ ꝉꝺuıRıs ꝙııc ɑn RıꝺıRe ó ꝼLóRens.

If we mark the unstressed vowels by a horizontal stroke, and the stressed ones when diphthongs or triphthongs, where possible, by the principal vowel sound of the combination, this stanza may be written in metrical symbols:-

$$- \acute{e} \; - \, - \; \acute{e} \; - \quad \acute{o} \, -$$
$$- \; \imath\mathrm{ɑ} \; - \, - \; \imath\mathrm{ɑ} \; - \, - \quad \acute{o} \, -$$
$$- \; \mathrm{ɑ} \; - \, - \; \mathrm{ɑ} \quad - \quad \acute{o} \, -$$
$$- \; \imath \; - \, - \, - \imath \quad - \, - \, - \; \acute{o} \, -$$

Here we have taken account of elision: thus, mo ċRɑoċɑö ıs is pronounced as mo ċRɑoċɑs. It should be noted too that in the second line there is a secondary accent with vowel correspondence after the first stress, which gives variety and beauty to the stanza.

The first stanza of Poem II [2] is -

> Ꝺo-ċuɑLɑ scéɑL ꝺo ċéɑs ɑR Ló mé,
> ıs ꝺ'ꝼɑȝ 'sɑn oıöċe ı nꝺɑoıRse öRóın mé,
> Ꝺ'ꝼɑȝ mo ċReɑc ȝɑn neɑRc mnɑ́ seoLcɑ,
> ȝɑn öRíȝ ȝɑn ꝙeɑöɑıR ȝɑn ȝReɑnn ȝɑn ꝼóȝnɑꝙ,

which in metrical notation is

$$- \; \mathrm{uɑ} - \acute{e} - \acute{e} - \acute{o} \, -$$
$$- \; \mathrm{u} \; - \acute{\imath} - \; \acute{\imath} - \acute{o} \, -$$
$$\acute{\mathrm{ɑ}} - \mathrm{ɑ} - \mathrm{ɑ} - \acute{o} \, -$$
$$- \; \acute{\imath} - \mathrm{ɑu} - \mathrm{ɑu} - \; \acute{o} \, -$$

The final stressed vowel is ó throughout the entire poem. In Poem III [3], which is a Cɑoıneɑö, the metre is the same as in I [1].

Ꝺɑ́n ꝹíReɑċ, in which some of Ferriter's poems are written, requires a fixed number of syllables in each line, four lines in each stanza, as well as a certain correspondence in sound between the final syllables of the lines, etc.

The principal kind of Ꝺɑ́n ꝹíReɑċ is Ꝺeıöıöe. Ꝺeıöıöe requires (a) the Rɑnn or stanza to be four-lined; (b) seven syllables in every line or ceɑċRɑꝙɑ. In counting the number of syllables, elision is taken into account. Elision of a vowel ending a word may take place when necesary, if followed by a word beginning with a vowel. If the vowel that follows be long, and the

11

preceding one short, elision of the short vowel is not general; (c) uⱥim or alliteration; that is, in each line, two words, of which neither is the article, possessive pronoun, or preposition, must begin with a vowel or with the same consonant. In compounds uⱥim is made by the initial letter, but particles like ᴅo and ʀo, when prefixes in compounds, do not count. Eclipsing letters, too, are not counted, nor are ḟ, ṡ, ċ reckoned in uⱥim. There are two kinds of uⱥim; ḟíoʀ-uⱥim or uⱥim cluⱥise, which takes place when there is uⱥim between the two final words of a line; and uⱥim ꝺnúise, when the uⱥim is between two words that are not final. Uⱥim ꝺnúise is more easily allowed in the first Leⱥċ-ʀⱥnn, or the seolⱥⱶ, that is, in the first two lines, than in the second Leⱥċ-ʀⱥnn or coṁⱥᴅ, that is, the last two lines of the ʀⱥnn or stanza, which require generally ḟíoʀ-uⱥim.

(d) Rinn and ⱥiʀᴅ-ʀinn, that is, the last words of the second and fourth lines (ⱥiʀᴅ-ʀinn), must be longer by a syllable than the last words of the first and third lines (ʀinn) respectively. For ʀinn and ⱥiʀᴅ-ʀinn compound words may be employed. Sometimes the word that ends one line has a prefix put before it in the next. (e) Coṁⱥʀᴅⱥⱶ, that is, the last syllable of each of the odd lines must agree with the last syllable of the succeeding even line in vowels and consonants of the same species. Two consonants to be of the same species must both belong to one of the following divisions into which the consonants are divided:-

(1) s, which stands alone.	(4) ċ, ċ, ḟ, (ṗ), aspirates.
(2) c, p, ᴄ, hard.	(5) ll, nn, ʀʀ, m, nꝺ, strong.
(3) ᴅ, ꝺ, b, mediae.	(6) ḃ, ⱶ, ꝝ, ṁ, l, n, ʀ, light.

The vowels are divided into – ⱥ, o, u, broad; e, ı, slender.

Coṁⱥʀᴅⱥⱶ slⱥn takes place when the vowels are the same, and the consonants of the same class; coṁⱥʀᴅⱥⱶ bʀisᴄe when the consonants are not of the same class, while the vowels are the same.

(f) Uⱥiċne requires a vowel correspondence between a word at the end and middle of the odd lines, and a word in the middle of the even lines respectively, that is, the vowels must be both broad or both slender.

(g) Ⱥmus is a correspondence between a word in the odd lines (at end or middle) and a word of the same number of syllables in the middle of the even lines respectively. The correspondence must take place not only between the vowels, but also the consonants.

In illustration of the ᴅeıbıⱶe Metre this stanza is taken at random from Ferriter:-

Ⱥʀᴅuıꝺ ᴅo ṁeⱥnmⱥ ⱥ ṁⱥꝺnⱥis,
Ⱥ ċúıʀ ᴅʀeⱥċ-ꝺlⱥn ᴅeⱥʀc-ṡⱥṁ-ꝺlⱥis,
Ⱥ ṡlⱥᴄ ḟıⱥl ıomlⱥn ı ꝺcⱥċ,
Ⱥ ıomʀⱥⱶ clıⱥʀ ıs ceⱥʀʀḃⱥċ.

Here we have obviously four lines and seven syllables in each, supposing elision in the first line where the two ⱥ's meet. We have uⱥim in the first line between ṁeanma and ṁáṡnais; and it is ṗíor-uaim or uaim cluaise. In the second line there is ṗíor-uaim between ꝺreaċ-ṡlan and ꝺearc-ṡáṁ-ṡlais. In the third line there is uaim cluaise between ṗial and iomlán, as ṗ does not count. In the fourth line there is uaim ṡnúise, though approaching to ṗíor-uaim, between cliar and cearrḃaċ. There is rinn and airꝺ-rinn in the words ṁáṡnais and ꝺearc-ṡáṁ-ṡlais, where the peculiar structure of the latter word is interesting; there is also rinn and airꝺ-rinn in the words ṡcaċ and cearrḃaċ.

There is coṁarꝺaꝺ slán, amounting to perfect rhyme, between ṁáṡnais and ꝺearc-ṡáṁ-ṡlais; and also coṁarꝺaꝺ slán between ṡcaċ and cearrḃaċ, as ċ and ċ are of the same species of consonants; amus between ṗial and cliar, as l and r are of the same species of consonants. Poem IV [4] is an excellent specimen of Ꝺeiḃiꝺe Metre, also V [5], XI [9]. Poems XVI [14] and XVIII [16] are also in Ꝺeiḃiꝺe.

Poems XII [10] and XIII [11] are in Rannaiꝺeaċc ṁór, which requires seven syllables in each line, each line to end in a monosyllable, and coṁarꝺaꝺ slán between the last words of the second and fourth lines; also amus between the last word of first and third lines, or some word in the middle of these lines, and some word in the middle of the second and fourth lines respectively. Here is an example taken at random from XIII [11]:-

Aṡ seo céime Ꝺé na noúl
Ar an cé ꝺá ꝺcuṡas ṡráꝺ
Croiṡ ċana 'ṡus seanṡ-ḃonn saor
Mala ċaol ꝺá noealḃaim ꝺán

in which the requisites mentioned are easily discerned.

Poem XIV [12] is irregular in metre.

Páꝺraiṡ Ua Duinnín (Dánca Ṗiarais Feiricéir, 1903)

Dánta Ṗiarais Ḟeiritéir

1. Mo ṫraoċaḋ is mo ṡaoṫ rem ló tú

[Capṫaoin Piaras Ḟeiritéar ccṫ. ar ḃás Ṁuiris ṁic an Ridire Ciarraiġiġ noċ ḋ'éaġ i ḃḞlónḋras i n-a ċapṫaoin i n-arm na Spáine. Is iomḋa ḋán ḋo cumaḋ le filiḃ cóṁ-aimsire Ṗiarais i gConnṫaeṫiḃ Ċiarraiġe, Corcaiġe is Luimniġ ar ḃás an ḋuine uasail Muiris Mac Ġearailt timċeall na bliaḋna 1646.]

Mo ṫraoċaḋ is mo ṡaoṫ rem ló tú,
A Ċiarraiḋiġ iṫ ċian-luiġe i gcoṁrainn,
Mo ċreaċ ṫ'ḟearṫ ṫar lear i ḃḞlonḋras,
A Ṁuiris ṁic an Ridire ó Flórens.

Cé mór an cráḋ ṫárṫuiġ roṁaṫ,
Ní raiḃ blas ná ḋaṫ ná ṫóirse air,
Ḋá ríriḃ gan ḟuiġeall gan ḟóbairṫ,
Fám ċroiḋe-se gur scaoileaḋ ḋo sceol-sa.

M'úiḋ leaṫ is mo ṡúil go mór rioṫ,
'San ċinneaṁain ḋo ċiorrḃaḋ na cóṁairle,
Mar ḋo ruġ an cnoc luṫ mar ṫóirċeas,
Is é seaċṫ mbliaḋna i nḋiaċair tórmaiġ.

An uair ḋo ċuala guais is gleo-niṁ
Síoḋḃán na ḋṫíorṫa ag cóṁ-ġol,
Ḋo sceimneas is ḋo ṡireas ḋo ċóṁḋaċ
Ar Ċríosṫ, is, fáiríor, níor ḋeonuiġ.

Ḋo ḃí Áine Ċnuic Áine ḋoṫ fóġraḋ,
Is bean ġuil ag Loċ Ġuir na ngleo-ḟear,
Caoi ag mnaoi binn i nGlinn Fóġra,
Is Ġearalṫ-ċaoi ag Seanaiḋ-ṁnaoi iṫ ċóṁġar.

Ḋ'aḋṁuiġ bean ḋo ċearṫ ar Eoċaill,
Bean siḋe ag Moiġíle ḋo ċóṁġas,
Uíḃ Mac Caille is Caṫraċ Móna,
Is Cinéal mḃéice ag ḋréim le ḋeoraiḃ.

The Poems of Pierce Ferriter

1. My Oppression And Distress In My Time

Captain Pierce Ferriter composed this poem on the death of Maurice son of the Knight of Kerry who died in Flanders as a captain in the army of Spain. Many poems were composed by poets contemporary to Pierce in the counties of Kerry, Cork and Limerick on the death of the nobleman Maurice FitzGerald. – *Note by Dinneen.*

[Maurice FitzGerald, Knight of Kerry, died in Flanders sometime in 1644-46. Traditionally, the Fitzgeralds or Geraldines were supposed to be related to a family of similar name (Gherardini) in Florence.]

[cRaocaim: I weary, abate, hunt down; saoc: distress; ló: (dative case of) lá, day, time, era; CiaRRaíòeac: person of the line of the Knight of Kerry; cian: a long time, a long distance; luiȝe: lying down, fall, decline; comRa: coffin; ⲣeaRc: tomb or grave.] You(r death is the cause of) my oppression and distress in my time/ O scion of Kerry, lying far away in a coffin,/ My destruction your (en)tomb(ment) overseas in Flanders/ Maurice, son of the Knight from Florence.

[cRáò: torment; cáRcuiȝ (mo cRoiòe): (my heart) fell; cóiRse: cuiRse, fatigue, affliction; ⲣuiȝeall: remnant; ⲣóbaiR: to almost happen; scaoil an sceol (scéal): tell the news.] Though great (any) torment that befell before you/ There was not taste or colour or (real) suffering in it/ Truly, without (*not even*) a remnant, without (*nor even*) a beginning (of suffering)/ In my heart until news of you(r death) was told.

[úiò: attention; súil: (eye or) expectation; ȝo móR: greatly; cinneamain: destiny; cioRRbaò: destruction; comaiRle: council (*perhaps* admonition, *perhaps a reference to* ÁRo-CómaiRle Cill Coinniȝ (*Confederation of Kilkenny*)); cóiRceas: offspring; oiacaiR: torment; cóRmac: giving birth.] I looked for you and hoped for you/ (Yet) fate was destruction of expectation/ (It was) as (if) a mountain had borne a mouse as offspring/ After seven years of labour pain.

[ȝuais: jeopardy; ȝleo: noise; nim: poison, virulence, rancour; síoòbean: fairy woman, banshee; cóm-ȝol: crying together; sceinnim: escape, spring, start; siRim: search, demand; cómoac: help(?); oeonuiȝ: grant.] When I heard the (warnings of) danger and deadly noise/ Of the banshees of the lands wailing in unison/ I started forth and implored help for you/ From Christ, but, alas, He did not grant (it).

[ⲣóȝRaò: announcing; ȝleo: noise, battle; caoi: crying, keening; Seanaò: *a Geraldine castle near Limerick*; ic cómȝaR: close to you, your own.] Anne of Knockany was proclaiming you(r death)/ And a keening woman of Lough Gur of the fighting men/ A lament by a sweet(-voiced) woman in Glenogra/ And a Geraldine lament by the (fairy) woman of your own Shanid.

[aomuiȝ: admit, acknowledge; cómȝas: closeness, relationship; oRéim: contending. *This verse refers to areas where relatives and allies of the FitzGeralds held sway.*] A (fairy) woman acknowledged your right in Youghal/ A fairy woman at Mogeely of your relatives/ (Also) the lands of Imokilly and Cahermona/ And Kenelmaigue contending in weeping.

15

Do ġlac eaġla ar Sacsannaċ sóġaṁail,
I ḋTráiġ Lí na ríġ-ḟear ó'r tóirṁis,
bean síḋe ḋoḋ ċaoineaḋ 'na ḋóirsiḃ
Ġur síl ġurab é a ḋíḃirt ḋ'ḟóġuir.

Ins an Ḋaingean níor ċaiġil an ceol-ġol,
Ġur ġlac eaġla ceannuiġte an ċnósta,
Ḋá n-eaġla féin níor baoġal ḋóiḃ sin,
Ní ċaoiniḋ mná síḋe an sórt sain.

bean síḋe i nḊún Caoin aġ brón-ġol
'S bean ḋútċais mo Ḋún-an-Óir-sa,
bean binn-scol Inseaċ Móire
Cois Féile fá éaġ óġ-scaċ.

Ar Sliaḃ Mis níor ċis an mór-ġol,
'S ar Sliaḃ fionnaġlan Fiolair na feola,
Ar Ċruaċaiḃ na Tuaċa ḋo tósġuin,
'S ar Ċnoc Bréanainn bréiḋ-ġeal bóṁar.

Ḋ'aiċniġeas ar an Eas-sín ḋtóirniġ,
'S ar an bḟuil-ċit ḋo ċuit 'san bḟóġṁar,
Ar séiḋeaḋ na réalta cóimeit,
Éaġ Ṡaosair nó t'éaġ ġur ḟóġair.

Ġiḋeaḋ a ġleacaiḋe, a ċaptaoin cróḋa,
Tiġ ḋo ḋamuin i n-aislinge sróill-ċuilt,
Ionnam féin ḋo ṡaoċ ġur ċoṁaiseas,
T'éaġ-sa tar éaġ Ṡaosair Róṁa.

Mór bḟile nár b'ḟile i ġcomaḋ,
I n-aṁras ar ḟeaḃas a n-eolais,
Ḋ'eaġla ná beaḋ ḋ'eaġna leo san
Marḃna naċ ba ṁarḃna cóir ḋuit.

Mór bḟaraire nár ṡatail ar Eoġanaċt,
Ba ċnútaċ leo ċlú is tú beo aca,
Lé'r b'anacraċ ḋul t'acḟuinne tórsa,
Ḋoḋ ċuma-sa ġo brúiġte brónaċ

[sóöáṁail: comfortable; cóirṁıs: you sprang (or descended) from. *The Geraldine castles in Tralee were in the hands of the English.*] Fear gripped the snug Saxon/ In Tralee of the noblemen you are descended from/ A banshee keening you in his doorways/ So that he thought that his own expulsion was being foretold.

[caigil: spare; ceol-ġol: melodious weeping; ceannaıöċe: merchants; cnósca: wealth (*cf.* cnuas).] In Dingle the musical weeping was not stinted/ So the wealthy merchants took fright/ [But] there was no danger to them in their fear/ Banshees do not keen their sort.

[ovċcas: heredity; bınn-scol: melodious cry; 'Oún an Óır: *Ferriter's castle*; Inıs ṁór: *the estate of the Knight near Listowel*; Coıs Féıle: *the area around Abbeyfeale.*] The banshee in Dunquin crying sorrowfully/ And the hereditary banshee of my 'Oún an Óır/ The melodious-voiced (fairy-)woman of Inishmore/ And (of the area) by the Feale because of the death of the young hero.

[cıs: abate; Slıab Fıolaır: Mount Eagle, *west of Dingle*; Cruaċa na Cuaċa: *Magillicuddy Reeks in the area known as* Cuaċ; Cnoc bRéanann: Mount *Brandon in North Kerry*; fıonnaġlan: bright-clear; cóscuın: began; bRéıo: robe, cover; bóṁaR: stocked with cattle.] On Slieve Mish the great crying did not abate/ Nor on shining Mount Eagle of the prey/ On the Mountains of Tuath it started/ And on brightly clad Mount Brandon stocked with cattle.

[eas-sín: rainbow; cóıRneaċ: thunder; fuıl-ċıoċ: shower of blood.] I knew from the rainbow with thunder/ And from the bloody shower that fell in the autumn/ From the projection of a comet from the stars/ That they foretold the death of Caesar or your death.

[ġıöeaö: yet; ġleacaıöe: champion; cıġ: came; 'oamuın: demon, spirit; sRóıll: satin; cuılc: quilt; saoċ: calamity; coṁaısım: I measure, guess.] Yet, O champion, O brave captain/ Your spirit appeared in a vision, (clothed in) a satin shroud/ (So that) in myself, I guessed a calamity to you/ It was your death, not the death of a Caesar of Rome.

[móR bfıle: many a poet; cóṁao: couplet; *note: the mss. give different versions of the first line*; aṁRas: doubt; eaġna: art; maRbna: elegy.] Many poets whose verses were unwritten (?)/ Doubting the merit of their knowledge/ In fear that they would not have the skill/ (to compose) an elegy that would be a fitting elegy for you.

[faRaıRe: soldier; sacaıl: step on; eoġanaċc: Munster (strictly, one of the divisions of land supposed to have been made among the sons of eoġan móR, King of Munster); cnúċaċ: anxious, jealous; anacRaċ: disagreeable; acfuınn: capability, power, substance; cóRsa: over them; cuṁa: sorrow.] Many warriors who never set foot in Munster/ Were envious of your fame when you were alive/ Who found your sovereignty over them disagreeable/ (But in) grief for you (were) dejected and sorrowful.

17

Mór maiġre ba maiġdean rómat,
Nár b'aiċreaċ ġur ċlas ví t'óg-ċur
Is tú gan ġangaiv gan meanga aċt von tsórt soin
Ó n-ar meallais a hanam 's a hóigeaċt.

Mór spéir-bean céavfaváċ i gcóiste,
Nár líogav aċt ós íseal beo oraib,
V'éis t'éaga fá bréivib sróill vuib,
Ag éav le n-a céile fóib-si.

Mór maoiċ-bean aoil-ċuirp is omr'-fuilt,
Vá gcíorav gan cíor aċt a gceol-ġlac,
Iar vtraoċav vos na téavaib órva,
'S a mbuiveaċas ag an ngaoiċ ar a hóige.

Iomva ríġ-bean míonla móvmar,
Fá ġlas vúnta i gcúil vá seómra,
Nár leig eagla carav vi glór-ġol,
Vov ċaoineav re hiovbairt a nveora.

I n-amras an marb nó beo ví,
An uair is mitiv léi a ċuigsint 'na hógċruċ,
Mar tug t'annsaċt anrioċt beo uirti,
An vtug vearb vo mairb níos mó ví?

Vo-ċïv mar vo víol an rós-vaċ
Ar mí-lí ba saoiliġe 'ná gósta
Is é a scaċán an scaċán scólta
Na laganaċ vó fras-sil a póir-vearc.

Vá silleav sin t'inneal is t'óg-ċruċ,
Vo ċreivfeav Béineas éirġe Avónis,
Vá bfaiceav tú it armaib vó-fulaing,
Bulcánus vot ġabáil mar ġleo-Mars.

Tug vo ġaisce vuit gairm is glóire
Tug fá veara i n-armaib t'óirneav
Tug gravam vuit tú a ġlacav ar vóiv ġil,
Rí Pilib is níor mistive a mórvaċt.

[mᴀɪ̵ʂʀe: great lady (*literally*, salmon); mᴀɪ̵ʓoeᴀn: maiden; ᴀɪċ̵ʀeᴀċ̇: sorrowful; cLᴀs
ʊí: heard by her; óʓ-ċuʀ: "young burial"; ʓᴀnʓᴀɪ̵ʊ: spite, deviousness; meᴀnʓᴀ:
deceit; óɪʂeᴀċ̇ċ: virginity.] Many a great lady who was a maiden before (she met)
you/ Was not dejected until she heard of your early death/ And you without guile or
deceit except to those/ From whom you won their soul and their virginity.

[spéɪʀ-beᴀn: fair lady; céᴀʊ̇ꞃᴀʊ̇ᴀċ̇: prudent, discreet; cóɪsċe: coach; Lío̵ʓᴀʊ̈:
entertained?, connected (with you)? (*lit.* decorated); ós íseᴀL: silently, secretly; beó
oʀᴀɪ̇b: while you were alive; ʊ'éɪs ċ'éᴀʓᴀ: after your death; bʀéɪ̵ʊɪ̇b: cloths; sʀóLL
ʊub: black satin, mourning cloth; éᴀʊ̇: jealousy; ᴀʓ éᴀʊ̇: vying.] Many prudent
beauties in coaches/ Who only met you discreetly when you were alive/ After your
death, in black satin mourning clothes/ Are vying with each other over you.

[mᴀoċ̇: tender; ᴀoL: lime; ᴀoɪL-ċuɪʀp: pale-bodied; omʀᴀ: auburn; ꞃoLċ: hair; ceoL-
ʓLᴀc: musical hand; ċʀᴀoċᴀʊ̇: exhausting, breaking; buɪ̵ʊ̈eᴀċᴀs ᴀʓ ᴀn nʓᴀoɪċ: freed
to the wind(?); ᴀʀ ᴀ hóɪʓe: in the manner of youth(?); perhaps óɪʂeᴀċ̇ċ: virginity.]
Many a fair-skinned gentle-woman, with her auburn tresses/ Being combed (rent)
with no comb but her musical (harp-playing?) hand/ After snapping the golden
threads (strings)/ Set free to the winds, in the style of the young (*her virginity gone
with the wind*(?)).

[ʀíʓ-beᴀn: noblewoman; míonLᴀ: gentle; moʊ̈ṁᴀʀ: well-bred; cᴀʀᴀ: friend, kin;
ɪoʊ̈bᴀʀċ: offering, sacrifice.] Many a gentle, well-bred noblewoman/ Enclosed in a
corner of her locked room/ Fear of her family (hearing her) preventing her from
weeping aloud/ Lamenting you with the offering of her tears.

[ᴀṁʀᴀs: doubt; ɪs mɪċɪ̵ʊ: it is time; óʓcʀuċ̇: youthful appearance; ᴀnʀɪoċċ: bad state;
ʊeᴀʀḃ: certainty.] Not sure whether she was dead or alive/ When she had to
understand, as to her youthful appearance/ How her love for you (when alive) caused
her to change form/ Did the certainty of your death affect her all the more?

[ʊo-ċí̵ʊ̈: she saw; ʊíoL: spend, fade; ʀós-ʊ̈ᴀċ̇: rose-colour; mí-Lí̵: bad colour;
sᴀoɪLɪʓe: expected; ʓósċᴀ: ghost, weakling; scóLLċᴀ: scorched, burnt; Lᴀʓᴀ́nᴀc:
furrowed; ꞃʀᴀɪs-sɪL: shed in showers; póʀ: family; póɪʀ-ʊ̈eᴀʀc: tender eye.] She saw
how the rose-colour faded/ Into a sickly colour suited to a ghost/ Her mirror was a
mottled mirror/ Etched by the showers shed by her tender eye.

[sɪLLɪm: I behold; ɪnneᴀLL: mien, deportment; ʊ̈ó-ꞃuLᴀɪnʓ: invincible; ʓᴀbᴀ́ɪL:
harnessing, dressing; ʓLeo: battle.] If she had seen your stance and youthful form/
Venus would have believed that Adonis had arisen/ If she had seen you in your
invincible armour/ (She would have believed that) Vulcan had fitted you out as Mars
(for) battle.

[ʓᴀɪsce: deeds, exploits; ʓᴀɪʀm: fame; ċ'óɪʀneᴀʊ̈: your advancement; ɪ n-ᴀʀmᴀɪb: in
arms, command; ʓʀᴀʊᴀm: honour; ʊ̈óɪ̵ʊ: hand; móʀʊ̈ᴀċ̇ċ: majesty.] Your deeds
brought you fame and glory/ (And) were the cause of your being advanced to military
command/ He gave you respect by taking your bright hand/ – King Philip, and he
might well do it, no matter (how great) his majesty.

Loinne, Laochas, Léigeann is Leoġantacht,
Oineach, anamōacht, eaġna is eolas,
Mire, míollacht, míne is mórtas
Ar altromas ġur ġlacais-se ġo t'chróchur.

Cia aġ ar ḟáġbais t'áille is t'óiġe,
An cneas ar ṡnuaḋ uain na bócna,
An leaca ar lí ġris an óiġ-lil,
'S an ōreach ar ōat na leaġ lóġṁar?

Cia ōár ṫiomnuis ionnṁas t'ór-ḟuilt,
Ciab ōíoġaċ na linnte lóġṁar
Léiṫreaċa ṁic Ḃéinis ōóiḋ-ġil
Ġaċ cuaċ is ġaċ ruainne ḋ ró-ḟaḋ'-ḟolt.

An ríġe reaṁar 's an ċealltar cóṁarōaċ,
An teanġa ṁall ar ġeall ġur ċoṁaill,
An troiġ ṫréan 's an taoḃ mar ṡróll ġeal,
An ionġa ċaol 's an béal mar pórpur.

Ḋo ċleasaiḋeaċt aġ marcuiġeaċt móir-eaċ,
Ḋo stairiġeaċt le sean-scríḃinn seolta,
I bpionnsa ġo n-ionnlas t'eolais,
Ó ōíġnit píce ġo bóiōcin.

T'ḟoistine nár bloḋaḋ le bóstuinn,
'S ōo banōaċt le bantraċt ḃeol-tais,
Ḋo ṡoirḃeas i n-am coōa 'ġus coṁroinn
Ḋo ōoirḃeas i n-am colġ is coṁlann.

Cia bus oiġre ōoō ṡaiōḃreas seoiōe?
Cia ōearscnas an ōán ḋ ōeoiḋ-si?
Ġan beiṫ is é let ṁéaraiḃ pósta,
Cleite ġé is tú aġ ōéanaṁ clóōa ris.

Cia ċuirfeas, mar ōo ċuiris, i mbeo-rioċt,
Aġ innsint t'inntleaċta is t'eolais,
Aġ tabairt teanġan ōi is anam a ōóċain
Soileaċ ṁarḃ nár balḃaiġ feoōaḋ?

[Loınne: strength; Laoċas: chivalry; Leoġantaċt: (lion-like) courage; oıneaċ: honour; anamöaċt: spirituality; eaġna: wisdom; mıre: mirth; míollaċt: mildness; míne: gentleness; móntas: pride, high spirits; altromas: nurturing; cró: enclosure; cróċun: putting in a grave.] Strength, chivalry, learning and courage/ Honour, virtue, wisdom and knowledge/ Good humour, mildness, kindness, spirit/ You received (these qualities) as a nurseling (and kept them) to your entombment.

[cneas: skin; snuaö: colour; uaın- foam; bóċna: ocean; Leaca: cheek; lí: colour; ġríos: blush; óıġ-lıl: young lily; öneaċ: countenance; leaġ: (precious) stone; lóġṁan: bright, valuable.] To whom did you leave your beauty and youth/ The skin (of) the complexion of ocean foam/ The cheek of hue of the blush of a young lily/ The countenance of the colour of precious stone?

[tıomnaım: I bequeath; ıonnṁas: wealth; cıaö: hair; öíoġaċ: channelled, wavy; lınnte: hollows; lóġṁan: precious; léıċreaċa: fetters; öóıo-ġeal: bright hand; cuaċ: curl; ruaınne: particle; folc: hair.] To whom did you bequeath the wealth of your golden hair/ The channelled locks of precious hollows?/ Fetters of bright-handed (Cupid) son of Venus/ (Are) every lock and particle of your very long tresses.

[Rıġe: forearm, limb; Reaṁan: plump, thick; ceallcan: face; coṁanöaċ: corresponding, likewise; coṁaıll: fulfillment; caoö: flank, breast, body; ıonġa: finger-nail; pónpun: purple, rose-coloured.] Of full limb, and countenance likewise/ The tongue slow to (give a) promise (except) for fulfillment/ The strong foot and the skin like bright satin/ The finger-nail narrow and the mouth rose-coloured.

[cleasaıöeaċt: skill, agility; eaċ: horse; scaırıġeaċt: knowledge; seolca: educated, requiring skill; pıonnsa: fencing; ıonlas: brilliance; öíġnıc: dignity, nobility, bóıocın: bodkin, dagger.] Your agility in riding great horses/ Your knowledge in old manuscripts requiring learning/ Your knowledge and brilliance in fencing/ From the nobility of the pike to the bodkin.

[foıscıne: composure; bloöaım: I shatter; bóscuınn: boasting; banöaċt: delicacy; banctaċt: woman-kind; beolcaıs: softlipped; soınbeas: sympathy, fellowship; coṁroınn: sharing; öoınbeas: harshness; colġ: weapon; coṁlaınn: conflict.] Your equanimity that was not shattered by boasting/ Your delicacy with soft-lipped woman-kind/ Your good fellowship in the time of sharing and dividing/ Your harshness in the time of weapons and battles.]

[oıġre: heir; öeánscnuıġım: I embellish; ıo öeoıö: after you; clóöa: letters.] Who will be heir to your wealth of jewels?/ Who will adorn the poem after you?/ Without – and it married to your fingers – / a goose feather, and you writing with it.

[soıleaċ: sally, willow; balöaım: I silence; feoöaım: I wither.] Who will put, as you put, in a state of life/ – by declaring your intellect and knowledge/ Giving voice (*song*) to it and a complement of being – / The dead willow, that withering did not silence?

21

Dá leo bannaiḃib aisciḋe córsa,
Is ba leaṫ féin an méiḋ nár leo san,
A mbuiḋeaċas sain is é ba stór ḋuit,
Is do buiḋeaċas-sa go léir a lón sin.

Níor ċaoḋaċ do ḋaonnaċṫ ḋó-ċleiṫ,
'S do baoḋaċas cléiriġ is comaiḋ-ḟir,
Níor éarais éarla ná óinṁiḋ,
'S níor aorais méirḋreaċ ná geocaċ.

Do rugais do roġa ba roġa go deoin dam,
Mar ḋíol i bḟíontaib 's i bḟeolṫaċ,
Mar ḋíol i gcíos-ḟleiḋ 's i gcóisrib,
I nḋíṫċeall tíorṫa ar do ṫórraṁ.

I nḋúṫraċt 's i gcuṁa do ċoṁ-ḟogais,
I gcaoineaḋ aois-ḟear is óig-ḟear,
I n-aṫṫuirse sean-ḃan gan ḟóirṫin,
Dearḃṫar 's i n-aḋċuṁa óg-ḃan.

Do haḋlacaḋ tú i n-aġaiḋ mo ṫóicim,
Is íslíġeaḋ pící ċum ḋóibe,
An druma ba ġlonnṁar glóraċ
'Na ós balb óc marḃ 'na ṫómas.

Muscaeiḋ is a nḋuib-béil fóṫa,
Halabairt 's a mbarra le fóḋaib,
Brataċa is iad ceangailte cnósta,
Láiṁ re talaṁ ḋá mannar gan mórtas.

Do ċlaiḋeaṁ ba ġníoṁṫaċ i ngleo-ḃruiḋ,
Lomnoċta ar onaċoin óig-ḟir,
Do ṁolárḋaċ ṡoláṁaċ is t'óir-spuir,
Go n-ionnlas ḋá n-iomċur róṁat.

Coirnéal gan oil-béim eolais,
Is captaoin ó gaċ glan-ċríċ d'Eoraip
Go stuamḋa i n-uain 's i n-órḋeir
San oirċill fá ċosaib do ċróċuir.

[bannaí: followers, bondsmen; aiscí: presents; córsa: beyond, also; buíðeacas: gratitude, regard; lón: sufficency, support.] To your people (you gave) gifts beyond (measure)/ And (they gave) to you that which was not for themselves/ Their goodwill was what you valued/ And your regard (for them) was their sustenance.

[taoðaċ: occasional, spasmodic; ðaonnaċt: kindness; ðó-ċleiṫ: discreet, concealed; coṁaíð-ḟir: men of verse, poets; éaraim: I refuse; éarla: earl, nobleman; óiṁiðo: fool, lowly person; aoraim: I satirise, scold, lampoon; méiroreaċ: harlot; ʒeocaċ: parasite, "waster".] Your quiet humanity was unstinted/ Clerics and poets held you in high regard/ You did not refuse the great or the lowly/ And you did not cast aspersion on your inferiors, men or women.

[roʒa: choice, will, highest achievement; ruʒaim: I win, obtain, bring forth, achieve; ðeoin: will, accord; ðíol: payment; cíos-ḟleað: rent(day)-feast; cóisir: wedding-feast; ðíċċeall: best effort.] You achieved the highest (reward), and it was a reward I concurred with,/: In recompense for the wines and meats (you gave),/ In recompense for your rent-feasts and wedding-feasts,: / The best efforts of the lands at your wake.

[ðúċraċt: zeal, earnestness; coṁ-ḟoʒais: people close to you, relatives; aċcuirse: affliction; ḟóirtin: shelter, aid; ðearbṫar: proven; aoðuṁa: great grief.] In the diligence and grief of your kin/ In the lamentation of old men and young/ In the affliction of old women (who are left) bereft/: it is proven: and in the great grief of young women.]

[tóicim: journeying; ðóib: earth; ʒlonnṁar: intrepid, fierce; ʒlóraċ: noisy; ós: mouth; balb: dumb; i ðtómas: for the sake of.] You were buried at my journeying (to you)/ And pikes were lowered to the ground/ The drum that was fierce and loud/ Kept silent because of your death (and) for your sake.]

[cnósta: bundled; mannraim: I unfurl, bundle] Muskets and their black muzzles (pointing) below them/ Halberts and their tips to the earth/ Flags and they tied and bundled/ Next the ground and they unloosed without pomp.

[lomnoċt: naked, unsheathed; onaċú: wolf, leopard; molároaċ: gauntlet; so-láṁaċ: handy, ready; óir-spuir: golden spurs; ionnlas: briliance.] Your sword that was effective in violent battle/ Unsheathed on a fearless young man/ Your ready gauntlets and your golden spurs/ Being borne brightly before you.

[oilbéim: reproach; uain: time, turn; i n-oiriċill: in harness, in readiness, awaiting; cróċur: interment.] There were colonels with knowledge beyond reproach/ And captains from every land in Europe/ Gravely in rank and in order/ In readiness for your burial.

23

Céad fear dec ġaoltaib feola,
I libré i nduib-éadaċ rómaib,
C'armus is é tarraingte ar ór-ḋaċ,
Ronnta ar an bfoġail-ċaċ bfórsaċ.

An uair do ġlacaḋ san talaṁ do ċoṁra,
Dá mbaḋ maidean lasaiġte an lóċrainn,
Do ḋéanfaḋ oiḋċe cíor-ḋub ceo ḋi
Le smúit an púdair do dóiġeaḋ ort.

Ġaċ saiġdiúir aġ deiṁniuġaḋ a eolċair
Aġ dúbláil cuṁa-ráḋ fá ḋó ḋuit
An túiseáil d'úr-báḋaḋ a ḋeora
Ġo dtiormuiġeaḋ le n-a osnaiḋib dóiġte.

Cérb é an ṁaidean an eaċtra tósġuin,
Is ġur ġearra ó'n eaġlais do nós-broġ,
Dob éiġin le méid an ṁórtais,
Baoḋaċas ar an ġcéir um nóna.

Naoi ġcaoġaid do ċléireaċaib corónta,
Deifireaċ i n-ionaraib órḋa,
Saġairt na salmaċ ġan coṁaireaṁ,
Is easbuiġ an deaċṁa, ar do ċórraṁ.

Muna mbeaḋ a méid do ċéidm dómsa,
Is ualaċ naċ ualaċ cóṁtrom,
Is maiċ do ċaoinfeaḋ mo ċroiḋe bróin tú
I ġcaoin-bers nár ṁílse aġ Óiḋid.

Ġideaḋ do b'éaġcóir, a ġrian-eoil nóna,
Naċ tú is aoirde ċaoinfinn d'fóḋla,
Naċ é is dílse ċaoinfeaḋ dóib tú,
Do Ṗiaras ba ṗiarla it póir-ḋearc.

Fá tú dam, an tan ba beo tú,
M'urraḋ síoḋa, mo scít tóirse,
Furtaċt m'éiġin, éide m'feola,
Coṁla m'áruis, fál mo ċórraiṁ.

[ᵹaol ꝑeola: blood relative; libre: livery; armus: coat of arms; ór-ṁaċ: gold coloured; ronnta: seals; ꝑoᵹlaċ: rapacious; ꝑórsaċ: violent. *Note: probably a reference here to the coat of arms of the Knight of Kerry.*] A hundred men of your blood relatives/ In black-clothed livery before you/ Your coat of arms and it delineated in golden colour/ Seals, and violent rapacious battle.

[Coṁra: coffin; lóċrann: lamp, sun; cíor-ḋub: jet-black; ceo: fog.] By the time your coffin was laid in the earth/ (Even) if it morning sunshine/ It would be turned into a haze of jet-black night/ From the smoke of the (gun-)powder that was fired for you.

[eolċar: loneliness, sorrow; túiseáil: convulsions?; úr-báṁaḋ: drowned anew; osnaḋ: sigh; ḋóiᵹte: burnt, scorched, wasted, scalded, cauterised.] Every soldier affirming his sorrow/ Re-iterating sad words again for you/ Convulsed by drowning anew his tears/ Until (they are) dried by his bitter sighs.

[tósᵹuin: began; broᵹ: home, castle; céir: wax, candles.] Though it was morning when the proceedings began/ And (though) it was (but) a short distance from the church to your customary home/ It was necessary, due to the extent of the ceremonial/ To resort to candle-light (as it extended) to evening.

[corónta: tonsured; ḋeiꝑireaċ: hurried, busy; ionar: tunic; salm: psalm, hymn, prayer; ḋeaċṁa: tenth part.] Nine fifties of tonsured clerics/ Busy in golden vestments/ Countless psalm-singing priests/ Every tenth one a bishop, at your funeral service.

[téiṁm: theme, subject of lament.] Were it not for the immensity of your (loss as) theme for me/ And a burden that is not a fair task (for me)/ It is well my sorrowful heart would lament you/ In tender verse that Ovid could not (match in) sweetness.

[ᵹrian-eol nóna: philosopher as bright as the mid-day sun.] Though it is an injustice, O noon-bright sage,/ That, in (all) Ireland, my lament for you should not be the deepest/ That my lament for you should not be the dearest/ (Since I am) your Pierce who was a pearl in (*of?*)your kindly eye.

[urraḋ: article, device, means; síoḋ: peace; scít: respite; ꝑurtaċt: help, comfort, relief; éiḋe: armour, clothing; coṁla: valve, door; ꝑál: protection, hedge; córraṁ: party, escort.] You were to me, in the time when you were alive/ My means of tranquility, my rest from weariness/ My relief from difficulty, the armour of my body/ The door of my house, the shield of my progress.

25

Mo ḋíon tuaiṫe, mo ḃuaċaill bó-eallaiġ,
Mo stiúir árṫaiġ ar lár bóċna,
Mo ṁaiḋe láiṁe i mbéarnain ḋó-ḟulaing,
Mo ċrann baġair 'san mbaile is tú i ḃḟlonḋras.

Mo ṫeaċ séaḋ, mo néaṁann nósṁar,
Mo ċnuas beiċe, m'eiṫe eiṫeoiġe,
Mo ġrian ġeiṁre, m'innscne óg-ḃan,
Mo ḋéar aille, m'airsiġ mór-scol.

Mo beiṫir ḋéaḋla, mo ċaor cóṁraic,
Mo ḋraġan lonn, mo Goll mac Móirne,
Mo ċuraḋ caoṁ, mo laoċ, mo leoṁan,
Mo ṁionn súl, mo lionn-lúṫ, mo lóċrann.

Do ṁalartais mo raċmas ar ró-ċeas,
Is do ḋíolais mo ṡaoirse let óg-ḋul,
Is tú anoċt mo ṫoċt 's mo ṫeo-ġoin,
Earr m'aoiḃnis is críoċ mo ġlóire,

Mo luain-ċreaċ, mo ġuais, mo ġleo-ḃruiḋ,
Mo ċneaḋ báis, mo ḃráṫ, mo ḃeo-ġoin,
Mo ṁíle mairg, mo ċealg, mo ċló-niṁ,
Mo ḋíle ḋonais tú, m'osna 'gus m'eolċuir,

Mo ṡileaḋ ḋéar, mo léan, mo leonaḋ,
Mo ġoin ċroiḋe, mo ḋíṫ, mo ḋeonċaḋ,
Mo ṡioscaḋ ball, mo ċall, mo ċró-lot,
Mo ċneaḋ clí do ṡíneaḋ i gcoṁrainn.

M'ár ḋaoine, mo ṁaoiṫ, mo ṁóir-ċeas,
Mo ḃraon allsa, mo ċanncar ḋrólann,
Mo ṁío-áḋ gan aoin-ċráḋ 'na ċoṁar,
Mo ḋíoġḃáil is mo ḋíoṫ-láiṫreaċ ḋó-innis.

Ḃa ṫaise ná an ḟearṫainn do ṡóḋantaċt,
Ḃa ḋaingne ná an ċarraig do ċróḋaċt,
Do b'ḟairsinge ná an Ḃanḃa do ḃeoḋaċt,
'S ba ċuṁainge ná t'úire an Eoruip.

[ᴏ́ıon: roof; cuᴀċ: countryside; eᴀᴌᴌᴀċ: stock; bó-eᴀᴌᴌᴀċ: stock of cattle; scıúıʀ: pilot; ᴀ́ʀcᴀċ: vesel; bóċnᴀ: ocean; beᴀ́ʀnᴀ: gap, chasm, position in battle; ᴏ́-ꝼuᴌᴀınʒ: insupportable, unendurable; cʀᴀnn: staff; bᴀʒᴀıʀc: threat.] My shelter in the wilderness, my stock-boy/ My ship's pilot in mid-ocean/ My hand-baton in unendurable difficulty/ My staff to threaten with at home and you in Flanders.

[séᴀᴅ: jewel; néᴀᴍᴀınn: mother of pearl; nósᴍᴀʀ: choice, beautiful; cnuᴀs: hoard; eıce: wing; eıceoʒ: winglet; ınnscne: speech, eloquence; ᴅéᴀʀ: tear, trickle; ᴀıᴌᴌ: cliff, rock, ᴀ́ıʀsıᴏ̇: veteran, champion.] My house of jewels, my beautiful gem/ My hoarding of bees (honey), my wing of winglets/ My sun in winter, my eloquence of girls/ My drop (of pure water) from the cliff-face, my champion of the academies.

[beıċıʀ: bear; ᴅéᴀᴏᴌᴀ: daring; cᴀoʀ: flame, glowing ember; ᴅʀᴀʒᴀn: dragon; ʒoᴌᴌ mᴀc ᴍóıʀne: *head of the Clann Móirne who slew Cumhal, father of Fionn of the Fianna, to whom Goll eventually submitted;* ᴌonn: strong; cuʀᴀᴏ̇: warrior; mıonn: crown, diadem; mıonn súᴌ: insignia envied by all; ᴌíon-ᴌúċ: fullness of vigour; ᴌóċʀᴀnn: lantern.] My brave bear, my flame of battle/ My strong dragon, my Goll mac Móirne/ My kindly champion, my knight, my lion/ My enviable prize, my fullness of vigour, my guiding light.

[ʀᴀċmᴀs: wealth, power; ceᴀs: grief, affliction; ʀó-ċeᴀs: great affliction; ᴅíoᴌᴀım: I expend; óʒ-ᴏ̇uᴌ: young passing; coċc: spasm; ceoʒoın: fevered wound; eᴀʀʀ: tail, conclusion.] You changed my well-being for great affliction/ And you laid waste my independence with your young passing/ You are tonight my convulsion and my fevered wound/ The end of my happiness and the finish of my glory.

[ᴌuᴀn: radiance, moon, Day of Judgement, *(also* loins, kidney, breast); ʒuᴀıs: peril, bʀᴀ́ċ: Last Day, fate, condition; mᴀıʀʒ: sorrow; ceᴀᴌʒ: sting, treachery; cᴌó: shape, form, body, *(perhaps* spike); ᴏ̇íᴌe: flood; eoᴌċᴀıʀe: homesickness, loneliness, grief.] My final destruction of the world, my peril, my bloody battle/ My death sigh, my final destiny, my life's injury/ My thousand sorrows, my betrayal, my body-poisoning/ My deluge of evil: you(r death), my sigh and my desolation.

[ᴅéᴀʀ: tear; ᴌéᴀn: woe; ᴏíċ: loss; ᴅeonċᴀᴏ̇: ruin?; sıoscᴀᴏ̇: dropping, shedding; bᴀᴌᴌ: limb; cᴀᴌᴌ: need; cʀó: house; cneᴀᴅ: (pain causing) groan; cᴌí: chest, ribs, body.] My shedding of tears, my sorrow, my wounding/ My wound to the heart, my loss, my ruin/ My ache in my side, my want, my destruction of refuge/ My sigh from the heart your stretching in a coffin.

[ᴀ́ʀ: slaughter, plague; ᴀᴌᴌus: sweat; cᴀnncᴀʀ: cancer, peevishness; ᴅʀóᴌᴀınn: entrails, heart; ᴅíoʒbᴀ́ıᴌ: scarcity, damage; ᴅíoc-ᴌᴀ́ıċʀıʒım: I utterly destroy, rout, confiscate; ᴅó-ınnıs: unspeakable.] My slaughter of people, my anguish, my great affliction/ My drop of sweat, my cancer of the entrails/ My ill fortune without any torment comparable to it/ My want and my unspeakable destruction.

[cᴀıs: soft; soᴏ̇ᴀncᴀċc: naivete; úıʀe: freshness, generosity.] Your good nature was tenderer than the rain/ Your courage was firmer than the rock/ Your spirit was more expansive than Ireland/ And Europe was slighter than your liberality.

27

Do leaġaḋ-sa mo leaġaḋ is mo leonaḋ,
Do ċailleaṁain ba ċailleaṁain daṁ-sa,
Ó ċailleas tú do ċailleas mo ḋóċas
'S ó's marḃ tú is marḃ cé beo mé.

Do ṡaoṫ rom-ṫraoċ is rom-ṫóirsiġ,
Rom-ṡaoṫ do ṫraoċaḋ is do ṫósdal,
Féiṫle na féile 's a fóir tú,
Mo ṫraoċaḋ is mo ṡaoṫ rem ló tú.

2. Do ċuala scéal do ċéas ar ló mé

Do ċuala scéal do ċéas ar ló mé,
Is ṫug san oiḋċe i ndaoirse bróin mé,
Do léiġ mo ċreat gan neart mná seolta,
Gan bríġ, gan ṁeabair, gan ġreann, gan fóġnaṁ.

Aḋḃar maoiṫe scaoileaḋ an sceoil sin,
Cás gan leiġeas is aḋnaḋ tóirse,
Aṫnuaḋaḋ luit is uilc is eolċair,
Ġríosuġaḋ teaḋma is treiġde móire.

Díoṫuġaḋ buiḋne críċe Fódla,
Laguġaḋ grinn is gnaoi na cóiġe,
Mar do díoġaḋ ar ndaoine móra,
As a ḃfearann cairte is córa.

Mór an scéal, ní féidir d'ḟólaing,
Méad ár nduíṫ do ríoṁ lem ló-sa,
Fuair an ḟéile léan 'na ḋeoiḋ sin,
Is tá an daonnaċt gaċ lae dá leonaḋ.

Ní ḃfuil cliar i n-iaṫaiḃ Fódla,
Ní ḃfuil aifrinn againn ná órda,
Ní ḃfuil baiste ar ár leanḃaiḃ óga,
Is ní ḃfuil neaċ re maiṫ dá ṁórḋaċt.

[Leaᵹaim: I lay low; beo: alive, in motion.] Your laying low is my laying low and my wounding/ Your loss was a loss to me/ Since I lost you I lost my hope/ And since you are dead, I am dead though (appearing to be) alive.

[saoċ: pain; cRaoċaim: I exhaust, destroy; cóiRseaċ: dejection, grieving, troubling; cóscal: cóiċeascal: pageant, display, parade, pride; péiċle: péiċleann: woodbine, leader; póiR: help, relief.] Your suffering is exhausting and troubling me/ Your destruction and your (funeral-)parade are belabouring me/ You were the chieftain of liberality and its defence/ You(r death) is (the cause of) my weakening and my pain in my time.

2. I Heard A Tale That Tormented Me By Day.

[scéal: story, news, report; ɒaoiRse: slavery, oppression; léic: neglect, failing, weakness; léiᵹim: liᵹim, I let, leave; cReaċ: frame, body; bean seolca: woman delivered *of infant (i.e. immediately after childbirth)*; póᵹnaṁ: serving, doing good, being useful.] I heard a tale that tormented me by day/ And by night put me in bondage of grief/ (It) left my body without the strength of a woman after childbirth/ Without energy, without thought, without mirth, without ability.

[maoiċe: softness, weakness; scaoilim: I release; aṁnaḃ: kindling, inflaming, beginning; cóiRse: torch (*perhaps* coiRse: tiredness, weakness); loc: destruction; eolċaiRe: homesickness; ceaṁm: pestilence; cReiᵹiɒ: colic, bitter grief.] The cause of weakness (is) the proclaiming of that news/ A case without healing and the commencement of weakness/ Renewal of destruction and evil and grief/ The incitement of disease and great pain.

[ɒíoċuᵹaḃ: destruction; ᵹnaoi: pleasure, affection; ɒíoᵹaim: I drain; peaRann: land; caiRc: charter, law; cóiR: right.] Destruction of the band of the land of Ireland/ Weakening of the happiness and pleasure of the province/ For our great people were drained away/ Out of their lawful and rightful demesnes.

[pulainᵹim: I suffer; ɒíċ: loss; Ríoṁaim: I count, enumerate; péile: hospitality, decency; ɒaonnaċc: mankind, humanity, human nature.] Awful the news, it cannot be endured/ The greatness of our loss to reckon in my day/ Decency was injured after that/ And the common people are being hurt every day.

[iaċ: meadow, region, country; neaċ: a being, anyone; móRɒaċc: greatness, magnificence, majesty.] There are not clergy in the lands of Ireland/ We have not masses or (religious) orders/ There is no baptism on our young children/ And there is nobody (worthy) of rank, no matter how pompous.

Créad do déanfaid ar n-aos óga,
Gan fear seasaiṁ ná tagarċa a gcóra,
Táid gan triaċ aċt Dia na glóire,
Is preasáil 'gá ngreasáil tar bóċna?

Greadán m'aigniḋ dearḃaḋ an sceoil sin,
Gaḃáil ġarḃ na n-eaċtrannaċ óirnne,
Maiṫ ḟios agam an t-aḋḃar far órduiġ,
D'aiṫle ár bpeacaḋ an tAṫair do ḋeonuiġ.

Dá mbeiṫ Tuaṫal fuadraċ beo againn,
Nó Feidlim do ċreiġidreaḋ tóra,
Nó Conn, fear na gcaṫ do ró-ċur,
Ní beiṫ teann na nGall dár ḃfógraḋ.

Cár ġaḃ Art do ċar an ċróḋaċt?
Nó Mac Con ba ḋoċt i gcoṁlainn,
Le n-ar scannraiġ clann Oilioll Óluim?
Is séan do Ġallaiḃ ná mairid na treoin sin.

Is léan do Ḃanḃa marḃaḋ Eoġain,
Tréin-ḟear fá ceile don ḃeoḋaċt,
Ní beiṫ neart tar ċeart ar ḟódaiḃ,
Ag na Ġallaiḃ meara móra.

Do ḃeiṫ neart is ceart is cróḋaċt,
Do ḃeiṫ smaċt is reaċt fá ró-ċion,
Do ḃeiṫ raṫ ar ar san ḃfoġmar,
Dá mbeiṫ Dia le triaṫaiḃ Fódla.

D'imṫiġ Brian na gcliar ón mBóirṁe,
Do ḃí tréiṁse ag Éirinn pósta,
Ní ḃfuil Murċaḋ cumasaċ cróḋa
I gCluain Tairḃ ba ṫaca re cóṁlann.

An tan fá láidir trá na treoin sin
Clann Cárrṫaiġ 's an Tál-ḟuil treoraċ,
Níor ṡaoileadar Ġaill dá ḃfógraḋ,
Tar tuinn nó i gcríoċaiḃ Fódla.

[seasaim: I stand, defend; casraim: I plead, dispute, bring to account; triac: chief; preasáil: pressing, compulsion; sreasálaim: I beat, strike, drive; bócna: ocean.] What shall our young people do/ Without a man for defending and representing their rights/ They are without a leader except God of glory/ And force driving them overseas.

[sreadán: heat, torture; sabáil: treatment; eaccrannac: foreigner; aicle: vestige; d'aicle: in the wake of, after.] The torture of my mind is the confirmation of that news/ The violence of the foreigners over us/ I know well the cause why (He) permitted (it)/ Because of our sins the Father allowed it.

[Tuacal, Ferölim, Conn: *kings of Ireland*; fuadrac: active; creiscoim: I wound, pierce, cause pain; tóra: pursuits; teann: force.] If active Tuathal was alive with us/ Or Feidhlim who damaged pursuing enemies/ Or Conn, the man who gave battle well/ The might of the foreigners would not be outlawing us.

[Art, Mac Con: *kings of Ireland*; Oilioll Óluim: *a king of Munster*; caraim: I love; docc: hard, strict; cómlann: conflict, contest; treon: strong, mighty.] Where did Art go, who loved courage?/ Or Mac Con, fierce in battle,/ Who frightened the clan of Oilioll Óluim?/ Happy for the foreigners that those strong leaders are not alive (now).

[Eoscan: *king of Munster, son of* Oilioll Óluim; céile: spouse; beodacc: courage, vigour, liveliness; mear: swift, *also* mad.] Woe to Ireland the death of Eoghan/ A strong man married to courage/ There would not be might over right in (title to) land/ With the big mad foreigners.

[Rac: success, prosperity, grace, favour; araim: I plough, cultivate (*cf. Latin, arare, to plough*); ar: tillage; triac: leader.] There would be might and right and heroism/ There would be power and law (held in) high regard/ There would be increase in tillage in the autumn/ If God was with the chiefs of Ireland.

[Brian Bóirme: Brian Boru; Murcad: Brian Boru's son, also king of Munster.] Brian of the clerics left the Bóirmhe/ Who was for a time married to Ireland/ Capable, brave Murchadh is not/ In Clontarf: he was a support in battle.

[trá: well (interjection); treorac: efficient; fósraim: I proclaim, outlaw.] It was a time, however, when those leaders were strong/ – Clan Carthy and the mighty Tál-breed – / They never thought that foreigners would outlaw them/ Overseas or in the lands of Ireland.

Atáid na Danair i leabaid na Leoġan,
Ġo seascair sáṁ ġo sáḋail seomraċ,
Ḃríoġṁar biaḋṁar briaċrac bórḋṁar,
Coiṁiġṫeac cainnteaċ sainnteaċ srónaċ.

Is é rún is fonn na fóirne,
Dá méid síc do-níd re ár bpór-ne
An dronġ bíos aġ ríoṫeaċ leo-san
Súġraḋ cluiċroe an ċuiċín ċróḋa.

Is truaġ lem ċroiḋe 'sis tinn dár ndreólainn,
Nuaċar Ċrioṁṫainn, Cuinn is Eoġain
Suas ġac oiḋċe aġ luiġe le deoraiḃ,
'S ġan luaḋ ar a tí do bí aici pósta.

Teaċ Tuaṫail monuar do tóirneaḋ,
Is Cró Cuinn ġan cuiṁne ar nósaiḃ;
Fonn Féidlim ġo tréiṫ-laġ tóirseaċ,
Laċ lúġuine ġo brúiġte brónaċ.

Acaḋ Airt fá ċeas ġan sóġċas,
Críoċ Coḃṫaiġ fá oġaim aġ slóiġtiḃ;
Clár Cormaic, fáid foirtil na ġcoṁ-focal,
Fá orċra lán d'foċram deoraċ.

Mo léan, ní hé tréine na slóġ soin,
Ná buirbe na fuirne ó Dóḃer,
Ná neart naiṁde caill ár ndóċas
Aċt díoġaltas Dé tá ar Éirinn fóo-ġlais.

Peacaḋ an tsinnsir, claoine an tsóisir,
Aiṫne Críost ġan suim na ċóṁall,
Éiġean bruinneall, briseaḋ pósta,
Craos is ġuid is iomaḋ móide.

Neaṁ-cion ġnáṫ is tár ar órdaiḃ,
Réabaḋ ceall is feall is fórsa,
Leiġean na ḃfann ġan ċabair ġan cóṫrom
Aġ saob-luċt sainnte is caillte ar ċóṁarsain.

[Oanair: Danes (=savages); seascair: comfortable, at ease, snug; sádail: luxuriant; seomrac: "roomy"; bóromar: full-tabled; srónac: nasal(-sounding?, big-nosed?).] The Danes are in the bed of the lions/ Snug, content, luxuriant, well-housed/ Lively, abounding in food, talkative, well-provisioned/ Foreign, noisy, greedy, twangy.

[rún: secret, intent; ṗonn: desire, predisposition; ṗoireann: team, gang; síc: peace; pór: race, kind; oronġ: team; réróceaċ: settling with, negotiating.] It is the plan and desire of the gang/ No matter what peace they make with our kind/ The party that is dealing with them/ (Are like mice) playing the game of the cruel little cat.

[orólann: gut; nuaċar: spouse, sweetheart; luiġim le: I am disposed to.] It is sadness to my heart and sickness to my entrails/ The spouse of Criomhthann, Conn and Eoghan/ Up all night abandoned to tears/ And no mention of the person who was married to her.

[Ceaċ Tuaċail, Cró Cuinn, ṗonn Ḟéiḋlim, lat lúġaine, Acaḋ Airt, Críoċ Ċobċaiġ, Clár Ċormaic: figurative expressions for Ireland; monuar: alas; toirnim: I humble, destroy, defeat.] The House of Tuathal, alas, was destroyed/ And the Seat of Conn without memory of traditions/ The Land of Feidhlim weak and exhausted/ The Meadow of Iughain beaten and sorrowful.

[acaḋ: field; ceas: grief, affliction; sóġaċas: pleasure, comfort; uġaim: harness, traces, tyranny; ṗáiḋ: prophet, seer, poet; ṗoirtil: mighty, able, patient; coṁ-ṗocal: synonym; orċra: act of destroying, decline, death.] The Field of Art is under affliction without relief/ The Territory of Cobhthaigh is under tyranny of armies/ The Plane of Cormac, great poet of synonyms/ In eclipse, full of the sounds of weeping.

[borb: fierce, rude, rough.] My sorrow, it is not the strength of those armies/ Nor the fierceness of the gang from Dover/ Nor the strength of enemies that lost our hope/ But the punishment of God that is on Ireland of the green sods.

[sinnsear: senior; claoine: perversity, corruption; sóisear: junior; aicne: commandment; coṁall: fulfilment; éigean: force, rape, atrocity; bruinneall: fair lady, maiden.] The sin of the elders, the corruption of the young/ The commandment of Christ, no interest in its fulfilment/ The rape of maidens, the breaking of marriages/ Greed and theft and excess of oaths.

[neaṁ-cion: disregard, scorn; ġnác: custom; tarr: belly, burden; saob: perverse, mad; caillim ar: I fail or forsake (somebody).] Neglect of customs and oppression of (religious) orders/ Destruction of churches and treachery and force/ Abandonment of the weak without aid or fairness/ By the foolish tribe (known for) greed and letting down neighbours.

Tréigean Dé le spéis i seodaiḃ,
Gléas le a séantar gaol is cómġas,
Géill do neart 's an lag do leonaḋ,
Claonaḋ breaċ 's an ceart fá ceo ċur.

Cioḋ tá an eang so teann ag tórmaċ
Fá láiṁ leaḃair na nGall so nóḋ againn,
Áilim Aon-Ṁac tréan na hÓiġe
Go dtigiḋ an ceart san alt 'n-ar cóir dó.

Is bíoḋġaḋ báis liom cás mo ċómarsan,
Na saoiċe sáṁa sásta seolta,
'Na dtír ba ġnátaċ lán do tóḃaċt,
Ite, vade, dá ráḋ leo-san.

Is gan aċt cáirde ó ló go ló aca,
Dá gcur uile i dtuilleaḋ dóċais,
Go mbeiċ fáḃar dá ḟaġáil dóib sin
Is gan ann sin aċt till further order.

Galar gan téarnaḋ is méala mór liom,
Greamanna daor-báis, cé táim glóraċ,
Scaipeaḋ ar an ḃféinn dár ġéill Clár Fóḋla,
Is Eaglais Dé dá claoċláḋ as órdaib.

Ta scéiṁ ġlan na gréine go nóna,
Fa éiclips ó éirġe ló ḋi;
Táid na spéarta i ngné dá ḟóġraḋ,
Ná fuil téarma ár saoġail ró-fada.

Fuair an cáirdeas spás a ḋócain,
Le luċt séaḋ ní géar an sceol soin;
Ní léir dam aoinneaċ ar m'eolas
Noċ do ḃéarfaḋ réal cum bróg dam.

Fágaim sin ar cur an Cómaċtaiġ
Aon-Ṁac Muire gile móire
As a ḃfuil ár n-uile ḋócas
Go ḃfuiġiḋ sib-se is mise cómtrom.

[ʒléᴀs: device, means; séᴀnᴀim: I deny, refuse, avoid; cóṁʒᴀs: "close person", relative; clᴀonᴀim: I incline, diverge, pervert; bʀeiꞇ: judgement, law; ceo: fog, delusion, humbug.] Abandonment of God through interest in riches/ – the means of rejecting kith and kin – / Giving way to might, and the wounding of the weak/ Perversion of law, and justice lost sight of.

[eᴀnʒ: track, land; ceᴀnn: strong; ᴀʒ ꞇóʀmᴀċ: developing, swelling; leᴀbᴀʀ: (*adjective*) long, tenuous, extensive; ᴀilim: I beseech; óiʒ: virgin; ᴀlꞇ: joint, knuckle, *also* condition, order.] Though this land is developing strongly/ Under the extensive hand of these new foreigners/ I beseech the great Only-Son of the Virgin/ That justice may come to the state that is due.

[bíoᴆʒᴀᴆ: start, sudden fit; cás: cause, case; ꞇóbᴀcꞇ: ꞇábᴀċꞇ, importance; *ite, vade*: move, go.] The trouble of my neighbours is a death-spasm to me/ The happy, satisfied, accomplished masters/ In their country, where it was natural (for them) to be full of importance/ "*Ite, vade*", being addressed to them.

[cᴀiʀᴆe: credit, respite, delay, procrastination.] And only respite for them from day to day/ Putting them all in more hope/ That favour might be found for them/ But it was only "*till further order*".

[ꞇéᴀʀnᴀᴆ: escape, recovery (*from sickness*); méᴀlᴀ: shame, loss, regret; ʒʀeim (*plural* ʒʀeᴀmᴀ, ʒʀeᴀmᴀnnᴀ): hold, bite, bondage, throttling grip; ᴆᴀoʀ: enslaved, condemned; ʒlóʀᴀċ: having speech; clᴀoċluiʒim: I change, oppress, destroy; ᴀs óʀᴆᴀib: out of (good) order? (*could be* ᴀ's óʀᴆᴀ: and (religious) orders?).] A fever from which there is no recovery, and a great sadness to me/ (I am in) the throes of a slave's death, though I (still) speak/ The scattering of the Fianna to whom (everybody in) the Plain of Ireland gave way/ And the Church of God being changed out of (proper) order.

[scéiṁ: overhang, verge, also appearance, beauty; ʒné: characteristic, form, appearance.] The pure beauty of the sun, to evening-time/ Under eclipse, from break of day/ The skies are ominously announcing/ That the term of our life is not too long.

[cáiʀᴆeᴀs: friendship, alliance; spás: reprieve, extension of time (as in paying a debt); séᴀᴆ: jewel, money.] Affection was extended to the end/ To monied people that is not bitter news/ It is not clear to me anyone I know/ Who could give me a sixpence for shoes.

[cuʀ: disposal, authority, jurisdiction.] I leave it so at the disposal of the Mighty (God)/ The Only-Son of great, bright Mary/ In whom is all our hope/ That you and I will get justice.

Is aiccim Íosa, Rí na glóire,
Mar is fíor gur críonas fógnas,
Soillse laoi agus oïḋċe ḋ'órḋuiġ,
Go ḋtigiḋ an ní mar šílim ḋóiḃ sin.

An Ceangal:

Gríosuġaḋ cneaḋ, laġḋuġaḋ ar neart, síoruġaḋ ar ċeas brónaċ;
Fíoruġaḋ ár ḃfear ḋo ġeiṁliuġaḋ i nglas, foillsiuġaḋ a n-aċt óirnne;
Críoċnuġaḋ ár ḃflaiċ ḋo ḋíoruġaḋ amaċ ar ḋruim tonn tar bóċna;
Ḋo ṁíon-ḃrúiġ laġ mo ċroiḋe ḋúr leasc re maoċuġaḋ ár nḋearc nḋeoraċ.

3. Iomḋa iorraḋ ag tulaiġ Tuaċail.

Iomḋa iorraḋ ag tulaiġ Tuaċail,
Iomḋa mór-ḃrat órċa uasal,
Is brat síoḋa fíor-ġlan uaine
Ḋo ċaiċ sí go groiḋe ḋá guailniḃ.

Iomḋa rioċt is cruċ ḋo ċuarḋuiġ,
Iomḋa aiċearraċ aiċiorais ualaiġ,
Iomḋa ḋoirḃeas, ḋoilġeas, ḋuairceas,
Is cúis faoilte is aoiḃnis fuair sin.

Iomḋa aċarruġaḋ ḋeacaṁail ḋuaiḃseac,
Ḋo rinne sí le cuiṁne a cuallaċt,
Is blaḋ bróin, ḋom ḋóiġ, is buan-ḃrat,
Ḋo ċuir uirċi an Ċorcra ċnuaisteaċ.

Iomḋa leanḃ lér caraḋ a nuaiḋ-rioċt,
Noċ ar alcuiġ a sealḃ go suaiṁneaċ
Is céile ḋo féaġaḋ a fuair-ċneas,
Ḋo ċaill sí go fíor gan fuasclaḋ.

Ḋearḃċar so ar a holc an uair seo,
Táinig anċruċ anacraċ uaisti,
Táirnig earr a háinis uaiċi
'S ḋo šíl fréaṁa a saor-ḋearc snuaḋ-ġlas.

[ɑɩċċɩm: I implore; cʀíonɑs: fast of three days; ᵱóᵹnɑɩm: I avail, suffice, perform, satisfy, am of use to; Lɑoɩ: Lɑe, *gen. of* Lá, day.] I implore of Jesus, King of Glory/ For it is true that devotion (to Him) prevails/ (He who) ordered the lights of day and night/ That that which I think (is right) shall happen for them.

The *Envoi*:

[cneɑᴅ: sharp pain causing a groan; síoʀuᵹɑᴆ: making permanent; ceɑs: affliction; ᵱíoʀuᵹɑᴆ: making certain; ᵹeɩṁlɩᵹɩm: I fetter, bind, chain; ɑċc: act (of parliament), law; ᴅíʀɩᵹɩm: I direct, guide; mɩon-bʀúɩᵹɩm: I crush, grind; ᴅúʀ: hard, withered; Leɑsc: sluggish, loath, reluctant; mɑoċuᵹɑᴆ: moistening; ᴅeɑʀc: eye.] The incitement of pain, the weakening of strength, the perpetuation of sad affliction/ The confirmation of our men shackled in prison, the proclaiming of their laws over us/ The extinction of our nobility that were ordered out across the waves, over the seas/ It crushed to weakness my slow, withered heart, with the moistening of our tearful eyes.

3. The Hill Of Tuathal Has Many Garments.

[ɩomᴆɑ: many; ɩoʀʀɑᴆ: *cf.* eɑʀʀɑ, article (of clothing), garment; Culɑċ Cuɑċɑɩl: the Hill of Tuathal, *a figurative term for Ireland*; ᵹʀoɩᴆe: spirited, generous.] The Hill of Tuathail (=*Ireland*) has (had) many (changes of) garments/ Many a great, golden noble mantle/ Many a truly pure green silken cloak/ Did she wear heartily on her shoulders.

[ʀɩoċc: guise, form; cuɑʀᴅuɩᵹɩm: I seek, examine, visit; ɑɩċeɑʀʀɑċ: alternative; uɑlɑċ: load, burden, obligation; ᴅoɩʀbeɑs: discontent, grief, anguish; ᴅoɩlᵹeɑs: distress, sorrow; ᴅuɑɩʀceɑs: sadness; ᵱɑoɩlce: = ᵱáɩlce?] She sought many guises and shapes/ Many alternatives and changes of burden (of clothing)/ Much grief, distress, sorrow/ And (also) found reason for welcome and happiness.

[ᴅeɑcɑṁɑɩl: difficult, troublesome; ᴅuɑɩbseɑċ: sorrowful; cuɑllɑċc: clan, company; blɑᴆ: renown, fame; ᴅóɩᵹ: likelihood; ɑn Coʀcʀɑ ċnuɑɩsceɑċ: the woman in purple who gathers treasures, *figurative for Ireland*.] Many a difficult, sorrowful change/ She made in the memory of her people/ (But) it is the name of sorrow, I am sure, that is the permanent mantle/ That the purple hoarding woman put on herself.

[cɑʀɑɩm: I love; nuɑɩᴆ-ʀɩoċc: fresh appearance; ɑlcuɩᵹɩm: I nourish, cherish, cultivate(?); seɑlb: property; ᵱéɑᵹɑɩm: ? *perhaps related to* ᵱéɑᵹmɑɩs *or* éɑᵹmɑɩs, loss, lack; ᵱuɑsclɑᴆ: deliverance.] Many a child (of hers) that loved her fresh appearance/ And that cultivated her wealth in happiness/ And (many a) spouse deprived (of the touch of) her cool skin(?)/ She truly lost without deliverance.

[ᴅeɑʀbċɑʀ: it is made definite; olc: misfortune, evil thing, damage; ɑnċʀuċ: bad shape; ɑnɑcʀɑċ: disagreeable; uɑɩscɩ: uɩʀcɩ, on her; cáɩʀnɩᵹ: finish; eɑʀʀ: end; áɩneɑs: pleasure; snuɑᴆ: appearance; snuɑᴆ-ᵹlɑs: fresh appearance.] Her misfortune is certain this time/ A disagreeable, bad form came upon her/ The end and finish of her pleasure came about/ And the roots of her clear, bright eyes shed (tears).

37

Ḟá éag mná a cláċt do truailleaḋ,
Tárla an tuile-se, tuisle gan tualaing,
Tárrtuigeaḋ a léan, a séan d'ḟuaċaḋ,
D'ísliġ a seol, a brón buaiḋeaḋ.

Deoraḋ a tréad, a tréan tuairceaḋ,
D'árdaḋ a ceas, a teas d'ḟuaraḋ,
Do ṁalartuiġ a dreaċ geal ar ġual-daċ
Is do ċuaiḋ i n-aibíd an-ċaoin uaṫṁair.

Créad is ciall don liaċ Luain seo?
Créad ḟá táid ár lá gan luaiċe?
Cliar ḟá seaċ, gan aire ár n-uaisle,
'S ar n-éigeas dá n-éaraḋ gan fuaraḋ.

Mairgréag Ní Ḃriain an Niaṁ nuaḋ so
Cneaḋ ḃeireannaċ an Éiḃir-ġuirt uaṁnaiġ
Álaḋ a báis bráċ a buaiḋre
Díle a donais, a doċma 's a dualaing.

A ṡluaiġ Éireann, éiġim is uaillim,
Ḟáċ ár ndoċair ní hoċras uaire,
Orċra í gan ċríċ 'ga ċruaḋtan
Is cneaḋ ṁarḃṫaċ ṁarṫannaċ buaiḋearċa.

Tógam d'aon-láiṁ aon-ġáir uaill-ġuirt,
Caoiḋeam a gcás tráiġte tuaimneaċ,
Ḟreagram Éire ár saoḃ-stáid ṡuan-tearc,
Is glacam congnaṁ na ndúl n-uaċtraċ.

Raċad-sa isteaċ go teaċ na truaiġe,
Is glacfad aibíd ḟaid-scís uaiċe,
'S ní ba feasaċ d'ḟear fala ná fuaċa,
Cia díne don dís ba duairce.

Do-ġéan oireaḋ re fiċe gan fuaraḋ
Do ċuṁa díoċra ríoġna an Ruaim-ḟuilt,
Caoinfead a ceas, basa buailfead,
Is ní beiḋ deor 'na deoiḋ im ḋuairc-ḋearc.

[cláċc: softness; clacc: garb, colour, *also* pleasure, satisfaction; cruaillim: I defile, corrupt; cuisle: hinge, stumble, fall, misfortune; cualanṡ: endurance, patience; cárcuiṡim: I rescue, deliver, defend.] By the death of a woman, her garb was defiled/ This flood (of tears) happened, an unendurable misfortune/ Her sorrow was preserved, her happiness repelled/ Her sail lowered, her grief won a victory.

[ḃeoraḃ: = ḃeoruiṡeaḃ, exiled; cuairṡim: I batter, smite; ceas: grief, affliction; ḋreaċ: countenance, appearance; aiḃío: habit, costume; an-ċaoin: (*opposite of* caoin, kind, pleasing); uaċṁar: dreadful.] Her herd was exiled, her strength destroyed/ Her grief was raised up, her warmth was cooled/ Her bright countenance was changed to the colour of coal/ And she adopted an unpleasant, dreadful shroud.

[liaċ: woe, expression of grief (sob, shriek etc.); luan: Day of Judgement, calamitous day; luaiċe: swiftness; seaċ?: *related to* seaċainc, shunning, avoidance?; éaraim: I refuse; puaraḃ: cooling, relief, rest.] What is the meaning of this cry of doom?/ Why are our days so tedious?/ Clergy shunned, our nobles disregarded/ And our poets refused unrelentingly.

[ṁiaṁ: a personal name, *also means* lustre, beauty, appearance; cneaḃ: wound; Éiḃirṡorc: *figurative term for Ireland*; uaṁnaċ: fearful, dreadful, terrifying; álaḃ: wound; bráċ: judgement, cause; buaíṙe: sorrow; ḃoċma: moroseness, impotence; ḃualainṡ: suffering, affliction.] Margaret O'Brien is this new appearance/ The final wounding of the fearful garden of Éibhir/ Her (*Margaret's*) death-wound is the cause of her (*Ireland's*) sorrow/ Her (*Margaret's*) flood of harm is her (*Ireland's*) glumness and suffering.

[éiṡim: I call upon, bewail, cry aloud; uaillim: I howl, entreat, weep aloud; oċras: sickness; uair: an hour; oċras uaire: short illness; orċra: withering, decline, death, extinction; marbċaċ: fatal, cruel, grievous; marcannaċ: abiding, continuing.] O band of Ireland, I bewail and entreat/ The cause of our harm is not a sickness of one hour/ It is a wasting without end to its hardship/ (And) it is a fatal wound, enduring, grievous.

[ḃ'aon-láiṁ: as with one hand, all together; uaill: a howl, wail; ṡoirc: bitter, sour, salt; cráiṡce: ebbed, drained, empty, desolate; cuaimneaċ: loud; saoḃ: perverse, foolish, paradoxical, mad; cearc: scarce, scant, stunted.] Let us make, together, a single cry, a bitter wailing/ Let us lament noisily their desolate case/ Let us speak out to all Ireland our perverse condition, with little peace/ And let us accept the aid of the Higher Elements.

[cruaṡ: the wretched woman (the metaphorical person, of many different mantles, who is the subject of the poem); aiḃío: habit, costume, shroud; scíos: weariness, fatigue, grief; pal: grudge, spite; ḃíne: generation, age, tribe, series, row, the young; ḃís: a pair.] I shall enter the house of the wretched woman/ And I shall accept a robe for long-mourning from her/ And no man of spite or hate shall know/ Which of the group of the pair of us is more sorrowful.

[puaraḃ: respite; ḃíoċra: intense, eager, passionate; ruaim-polc: red hair.] I shall accomplish as much as twenty (people) without respite/ Of intense grieving for the red-haired noblewoman (*Margaret*)/ I shall lament her affliction, I shall wring my hands/ And, after her (death), there will not be a tear (left) in my sad eyes.

39

Créad nać díoċruaġ an ḟíon-ġruaḋ uain-ġeal,
'S a ḋá reaṁar-ṡúil seaḃacaṁail snuaḋ-ġlas,
A ḋá ṁaol-ġlúin aolaṁail ḟuar-ġlan,
'S a ḋá tirim-ċroiġ silte 'san tuama.

Mo ḃíoḋġaḋ bróin, mo ḃreoḋ, mo ḃuain-ċeas!
Mo ḋiḃle déar, mo léan, mo luain-ċreaċ!
Ġaol na riġte an Daoil dár dualġas,
Fuil araḋ-ḟlaiċ Seanaḋ na sluaiġte.

Caoinfeaḋ dreasa an dreaċ-ġeal dual-ċas,
Is caoinfeaḋ finn-ċriaḋ rí-Ḃriain ruaġṁair,
Ḃan-ua bola Ḃloḋ na buan-ḃla,
Pór príoṁ-ḟlaiċ na ḃfíon-ḟleaḋ ḃfuarċa.

Maiġre soineannḋa Sionann na suan-ṡreaḃ,
Uḃall cuṁra d'úir-ḟḃ d'uas-Ċais
Cnú do collaib ġan ċonċlainn ġuais-ḃeart,
Préaṁ do pailm ġlais Teaṁraċ Tuaċail.

Cé leor do ċráḋ cáiċ a cruaḋ-ġoin
Mairġréaġ Ní Ḃriain fá iaḋaḋ uaiġe,
Táiniġ doċar don tsolais-ġein tsuaiċnḋ
Is mó dáiḃ 'ná a bás do ḃuain-ċreaċ.

Táiniġ di ġan ioċ ar ċuar-ġort,
Aimrḋ dá héis ġaċ craoḃ cnuasaiġ,
Atá 'na diaiḋ an ġrian 'na ġual dub,
Agus an ṁuir 'na fuil ġo fuaisneaċ.

D'ḟáġaib i mbrón Fóola fuaiġte,
Do clóḋaḋ aoiḃneas naoiṁ-ġuirt Nuaḋat,
Tánġus ré 'na Céḋeaċ cuantaċ,
Táiniġ treiġiḋ is teiḋm 'na tuairim.

Beaġ an iongnaḋ tuirse is truaiġe,
'S a liaċt mór-ḟlaiċ bróḋṁar buannaċ,
Is rí naċarḋa, dreaċ-ioḋan, duasṁar,
Ruġ an t-éaġ i mbéal a buaiḋte.

[cRéaꝃ: why; ꝃíocRuaʒ: ꝃíol cRuaıʒe, object of pity; ʒRuaꝃ: cheek; ꝼíon-ʒRuaꝃ: ꝼıonn-ʒRuaꝃ, fair cheek; uaın: foam; Reaṁar: fat, wide; seaḃac: hawk, champion, hero; seaḃacaṁaıl: hawk-like, heroic, noble; snuaꝃ-ʒlas: bright-surfaced; maol: bald, bare; maol-ʒlún: smooth knee (*Dineen: round knee*); aolaṁaıl: lime-like, white, pale; cıRım: dry, sere, crisp, clean; sılım: shed, bestow, deposit.] Why is her fair cheek, white as foam, not a cause of sorrow/ And her two full eyes, noble, bright-looking/ Her two smooth knees, lime-white, fresh-pure/ And her two pure feet, deposited in the tomb.

[bíoꝃʒaım: I rouse, startle, become excited; bReoꝃaꝃ: act of sickening, enfeebling, crushing; ꝃıble: ꝃíle, flood; luan: Day of Judgement; cReaċ: destruction; Ꝃaoıl: kingship of Thomond? (Ꝃál ʒCaıs, the clan or territory of Cas (a king of Thomond)); ꝃualʒas: duty, reward, inheritance; aRaꝃ-ꝼlaıċ: aRꝃ-ꝼlaıċ, high nobility.] My inducement to sorrow, my sickening, my permanent affliction/ My flood of tears, my sorrow, my final destruction of the world/ Kin of the kings whose inheritance was Thomond (?)/ Blood of the high nobles of Shanid of the hosts.

[ꝃReas: a bout, turn, course; ꝃual: tress, lock; cRí: body; cRıaꝃ: earth, earthly body; Ruaʒṁar: pursuing, routing; ua: descendant; bol: art, skill; blaꝃ: renown, fame; póR: seed, race, kin.] I shall lament the doings of (lady of) fair appearance (and) wavy tresses/ And I shall lament the beautiful descendant of great Brian of the victories (*Brian Boru*)/ The artistic female descendant of Blod (*son of Cas*) of lasting renown/ The seed of the premier chieftains of the fresh wine-feasts.

[maıʒRe: salmon, *figurative term for* great lady; soıneanꝃa: happy; sReaḃ: gush, stream, current, drop; ꝼıꝃ: wood, *figurative for* clan; cnú: nut; coll: hazel; conċlann: equal, rival, comparison; ʒuaıs-ḃeaRc: dangerous deed.] Blissful salmon of Shannon of the quiet streams/ Fragrant apple of the fresh wood of noble Cas (*king of Thomond, descendant of Brian Boru*)/ (Who was) a nut of hazel, without equal in dangerous deeds/ Root of the palm (who was) Tuathal (who built) Tara.

[ıaꝃaım: I enclose; suaıċnıꝃ: remarkable, conspicuous; solasʒeın: source of light (*or* bright offspring?), great lady; ꝃáıb = ꝃóıb.] Though sufficient for the torment of all (was) her cruel wounding/ Margaret O'Brien enclosed in a tomb/ There came harm to the famous lady/ That was greater to them than her death that permanently destroyed (them).

[ıoċ: corn; cuaR: land; aımRıꝃ: arid, unfruitful; ꝼuaısneaċ: skittish, tumultuous.] As a result of her (death) there was not corn in the fields/ Every laden bough was unfruitful/ After her (death) the sun is as black as coal/ And the sea is in bloody tumult.

[ꝼuaıʒce: stitched, ensnared; clóꝃaım: I alter, change; naoıṁ-ʒuıRc Nuaꝃac: figurative term for Ireland; cánʒus Ré: cánʒaċas léı, there came against her; 'na CéRꝃeaċ cuancaċ: in her (land of) Keady of (many) harbours; cReıʒıꝃ: pain, pang; ceꝃóm: fit, spasm; cuaıRım: nearness to; ına cuaıRım: close up to her, upon her.] Ireland was left ensnared in sorrow/ The happiness of the holy field of Nuadhat was changed/ (Fate?) came against her in her land of Keady of the harbours/ Calamity and disease have come upon her.

[lıaċc: a great number; a lıaċc: so many; buannaċ: martial; naċaRꝃa: snakelike, venomous, ferocious; ꝃeaċ: countenance; ıoꝃan: pure, clear; ꝃuasṁar ?= ꝃuaꝃṁar: laborious, toilsome? or gift-bestowing?] Little wonder (there is) weakness and sorrow/ And so many great chiefs, proud and martial/ And fierce kings, of clear countenance, diligent/ That death took at their moment of victory.

41

Níor ċaill sí 's is fíor naċ fuair sin
Ᵹan a brat ar ᴅaċ a ᴅualais,
ᴅearḃaᴅ so 's naċ fo-ċneaᴅ fuaras
Ᵹurab iomᴅa iorraᴅ aᵹ Tulaiᵹ Tuaċail.

4. Moċean ᴅ'altrom an oirḃeirt

(ᴅ'Eamonn mac ᴅomnaill Ṁic an ᴅaill ᴅo ċuᵹ cláirseaċ ᴅó.)

Moċean ᴅ'altrom an oirḃeirt,
Ionṁain a ᵹeis ᵹníoṁ-oirᴅirc,
Cosc feirᵹe 'ᵹus fola soin,
Roᵹa ᵹaċ ceirᴅe an ċearᴅ-soin.

Re mac ᴅóṁnaill ṁic an ᴅaill
ᴅuain-ḃeanas bríᵹ a ᴅtaᵹraim,
Aonᴅuine an uair-se ᴅo ċin
Aoᴅaire uaisle is oiniᵹ.

Éamonn ᴅúileaċ mac an ᴅaill
Rún bronntaċ briaċar fortaill,
ᴅalta is ᴅeaᵹ-oiᴅir na nᴅall
Altra an ear-oiniᵹ Éamonn.

Fuaras ó ṁac mic an ᴅaill
Cláirseaċ alLánaċ álainn,
Seoᴅ buan breac-lonaċ buiᴅe,
Ealtonaċ nuaᴅ neaṁᴅaiᴅe.

A coṁmaiċ ᴅo ċruit ṡeanma
Ní fuair triaċ ná tiᵹearna,
Móir-ċréaᴅaċ cean is creaċ,
An bean óir-ċéaᴅaċ áiseaċ.

Ní maoiᴅeaṁ ᵹo méiᴅ mearḃaill,
Ní fuair éin-rí ᴅ'Éireanncaib
A coṁmór nó a coṁmaiċ sin,
ᴅonnóᵹ na bfonnaiċ bfriċir.

[ouᴀL: that which is natural, hereditary, customary or expected; ꝼo-ċneᴀö: minor wound.] She (*Ireland*) did not lose (a leader), and truly she did not find one/ Without her cloak being of the customary colour/ Confirmation it is that it was not a minor wound I received/ That the Hill of Tuathal has many mantles.

4. Greeting To The Guardian Of The Generous Deed

To Eamonn son of Donal son of the Blind Man, who gave him a harp.

[The townland of Ballymacadoyle (ᵬᴀıLe ṁıc ᴀn ᵬᴀıLL, Town of the son of the Blind Man) near Dingle was also known as Harperstown.]

[moċeᴀn: "my affection", a term of greeting; ᴀLᴄᴿom: nursing, fosterage; oıᴿᵬeᴀᴿᴄ: good deed; ıonṁᴀın: dear, beloved; ꝣeıs: ?= ꝣeᴀs, injunction, spell; oıᴿöeᴀᴿc: illustrious, noble; ceᴀᴿᴅ: trade, habit.] My regards to the guardian of generosity/ Beloved his customary way of noble deeds/ The restraint of anger and (bad) blood (*or bloodshed*?) it is/ The greatest of all trades is that trade.

[beᴀnᴀım: I cut, strike, carry out; bᴿíꝣ: power, virtue, meaning; cınnım: I progress, surpass, excel; ᴀoöᴀıᴿe, shepherd, herdsman, pastor, guard; oıneᴀċ: honour, mercy.] To the son of Donal, son of the Blind Man,/ Who always achieves virtue, I refer/ The one person, of this time, who excels/ The protector of nobility and honour.

[ᴅúıL: desire, longing, appetite, fondness; ᴿún: secret, mystery, riddle; bᴿonnᴄᴀċ: generous, giving; ꝼoᴿᴄᴀıLL: strong, powerful; ᴀLᴄᴿᴀ: nourisher, nurse, foster-father (*cf.* bᴀn ᴀLᴄᴿᴀ, nurse); eᴀᴿ-oıneᴀċ: = oıᴿ-oıneᴀċ, great virtue.] Passionate Eamonn, son of the Blind/ Generous in secrets, mighty in words/ The pupil and good heir of the blind (ancestors)/ The nurturer of great virtue is Eamonn.

[ᴀLLᴀ́nᴀċ: ? (ᴀLᴀ = eᴀLᴀᴅᴀ, craft, skill); Lonᴀım: I blush?; eᴀLᴄonᴀċ: = ıoL-ᴄónᴀċ, of many sounds; neᴀṁöᴀᴿᴅe: heavenly.] I received from the son of the son of the Blind/ A beautiful, skillfully-made(?) harp/ A lasting gem, speckled red and yellow/ Many-tuned, new, heavenly.

[seᴀnmᴀ: *genitive of* seınm; ᴄᴿıᴀċ: leader; ceᴀn ıs cᴿeᴀċ: "love and plunder"?, *referring to riches obtained by* fair means or foul?; ᴀıseᴀċ: convenient, useful.] An equally good harp for playing/ Was not obtained by leader or lord/ Of great herds, obtained by fair means or foul/: The useful gold-strung lady!

[meᴀᴿᵬᴀLL: confusion, frenzy; ᴅonnóꝣ: brown lady; ꝼonnᴀıċ: tunes, airs; ꝼᴿıċıᴿ: eager, earnest, intense.] It is not boasting (but) to the extent of my frenzy (of gratitude)/ Not one king of the Irish got/ So great or so good (an instrument)/ – Brown lady of the intense music!

Ní fuair Maine ná Mog Néro,
Ní fuair Laogaire a Leitéro,
Ní fuair Niall do noct don mil,
Ní fuair Brian ná Corc Caisil

Instruim oirdearc uigte fonn,
Éin-iongantas fiad Fréamann,
Dé Dannanac doilbte dil
'S bé Manannaċ gcoirċe gceirdig.

Is binn allṁurda aṁra
A géimeanna geanaṁla,
An éaċt-farránaċ foirbte
Dréaċt-allánac dearscnoróte.

Eoċair an ceoil 's a ċoṁla,
Ionnṁus teaċ na healadna,
An Éireannaċ gasta glan,
Géimeannaċ blasta biadṁar.

Aos fíor-galair, fir gonta,
Codlaid ris an gclár ċorcra,
An beo-badb don bróin do bris
Ceol-adb an óil 's an aoibnis.

Fuair corr a cnuas-ċoill i nAoi
Is láṁ-ċrann i Lios Seantraoi
Dreastaċ maoċ-lonn na gcleas gcorr
Is caoṁ-ċom ó Eas Éagonn.

Fuair mac Sitduill dá suideaċt
Fuair Catal dá ceardaideaċt
Is fuair Deannglan, mór an mod,
A ceanglad d'ór 's a hionnlod.

Maiṫ a hóir-ċeard eile sain,
Partalón mór mac Ċatail,
Cláirseaċ an óir 's na n-allán,
Dóig naċ práisneaċ Partolán!

[mᴀıne, moᵹ Néıꝺ, Lᴀoᵹᴀıʀe, nıᴀll, Coʀc: *various leaders*. Coʀc mᴀc Luᵹᴀıꝺ *was a king of Munster who built a fort in Cashel*; noᴄᴄᴀım: I uncover, manifest, reveal; mıl: honey, sweetness, excellence; ꝺo noᴄᴄ ᴀn mıl: who manifested excellence(?), *perhaps a reference to some earlier poem or story*.] Maine or Mogh Néid did not get (such)/ Laoghaire did not get its like/ Niall, who manifested excellence, did not get (such)/ Brian did not get (such), nor Corc of Cashel.

[ınꞩᴄʀuım: instrument; oıʀꝺeᴀʀc: splendid, excellent; uıᵹım: I sound (*e.g. the bottom of a river*); éın-ıonᵹᴀnᴄᴀꞩ: the unique wonder *or* miracle; ꝼıᴀꝺ: wood; ꝼʀéᴀṁᴀnn: a hill in Westmeath; ꝺé ꝺᴀnnᴀnᴀᴄ: related to the Tuatha Dé Dannan; fairy-like, magical; ꝺoılꞆım: I transform, cast under a spell; ꝺıl: dear, beloved; Ꞇé: woman, fairy, Muse; mᴀnᴀnnᴀᴄ: related to Manannan of the Tuatha Dé Dannan, fairy-like, magical; coıʀᴄe?: music?; ceıʀꝺeᴀᴄ: artistic.] Splendid instrument, getting to the profoundest depths of (musical) airs/ The unique wonder of the wood of Fréamhann/ De Dannanian, magical, sweet/ And fairy muse of artistic music.

[ᴀllṁuʀꝺᴀ: foreign, strange, exotic; ᴀṁʀᴀ: noble, wonderful; ᵹéım: lowing (of cows), cry; ᵹeᴀnᴀṁᴀıl: lovable; éᴀᴄᴄ: deed; ꝼoʀʀᴀnᴀᴄ: violent, vigorous; ꝼoıʀꞆᴄe: finished, perfect; ꝺʀéᴀᴄᴄ: song, poem; ᴀllᴀnᴀᴄ: skilled?; ꝺeᴀʀꞩᴄnuıᵹım: I transcend, excel.] They are sweet, exotic, wonderful/ Its lovable cries/ (This) vigorous, perfect achievement/ (Of) artistic, transcendent music(-making).

[comlᴀ: valve, door; ıonnṁᴀꞩ: wealth, riches; eᴀlᴀꝺᴀın: art; ᵹᴀꞩᴄᴀ: ingenious, clever; ᵹlᴀn: clean, bright, complete, exact; bıᴀꝺṁᴀʀ: nourishing.] The key of music and its doorway/ The riches of the house of art/ The clever, precise Irishwoman!/ Musical, tasty, sustaining!

[clᴀʀ coʀcʀᴀ: the purple board, the noble timber, *i.e. the harp*; bᴀꝺb: scald crow, battle goddess, female fairy, (ꝺᴀꝺb *is a banshee or war-goddess who hovers over battle-fields inspiring the fighters to the madness of battle*); who ; ᴀꝺb: (musical) instrument.] People (suffering from) severe diseases, (or) men who are injured/ They get to sleep with this noble timber/ The lively fairy-goddess who defeats sorrow/ The musical instrument of drinking and enjoyment.

[coʀʀ: harmonic curve or cross-tree of harp; cnuᴀꞩ-coıll: flourishing wood; ᴀoı: Magh nAoi in Roscommon; lᴀṁᴄʀᴀnn: front pillar of harp; bʀeᴀꞩᴄᴀᴄ: lively, merry; mᴀoᴄ: soft, gentle; lonn: strong, ardent, rapturous; coʀʀ: odd, unusual; com: waist, cavity, central part of harp?; eᴀꞩ éᴀᵹonn: in the mouth of the River Erne, in Donegal.] Its cross-tree was found in the bountiful forest of Magh nAoi/ Its front pillar (was found) in Lios Seantraoi/ – Lively, gently ardent (instrument of) rare features:/ And its beautiful central part (?) (came) from Eas Éagonn.

[ꝼuᴀıʀ ꝺe: accomplish?; ꞩuıꝺeᴀᴄᴄ: layout, design; ceᴀʀꝺᴀıꝺeᴀᴄᴄ: artisanship, manufacture; moꝺ: manner, condition, work, respect, honour; ınnlıᵹım: I prepare, set up, operate, *perhaps* ıonnloꝺ: inlay work?] Mac Sithdhuill accomplished its design/ Cathal accomplished its construction/ And Beannghlan, great honour (to him)/ (Accomplished) its gold bindings and its inlay.

[óıʀ-ceᴀʀꝺ: goldsmith; ᴀllᴀn?: *related to* eᴀlᴀıꝺe (art)?; pʀᴀꞩ: brass; pʀᴀıꞩneᴀᴄ: worker in brass?; pʀᴀıꞩeᴀᴄ: porridge, mess, imbroglio; perhaps some punning here.] Good – that other goldsmith –/ great Parthalon son of Cathal/ The harp of gold and artistry(?)/ For sure, Partholon is not a brass-worker!

45

Is í ba ċlos cian ó ṡoin,
Ag spreagaḋ spriḋe Sauil,
Go cruiṫ gcaoṁ gcailm-ċeannaċ ḃḟionn,
Go sailmċeaḋlaċ saor séisḃionn.

Cian ó ḋian-ċor Ḋolḃ is Sanḃ
An armacaċ, an oll-aḋḃ,
Ḋreaċ neaṁ-ḋub Gaoiḋealta ġlan
Ḋeallraḋ ḋraoiḋeaċta a ḋealḃsan.

Mongán is mac an Ḋagḋa,
Ḋias il-ġeasaċ ealaḋna,
Ḋá gcaoil-ḟéagsain a ceol so
Ḟá ṁeor gcaoin-éascaiḋ gcuḃra.

Ḋíol na néaṁḋa Nioclás Ḋall
A ḃíol-sa an ċruiṫ ċonċlann,
An ḋall-sa ḋisi ḋoir
Is isi ḋ'annsa an oirḟḋoiġ.

Éin-ní i gconċlann a ceoil uill
Níor ċóir aċt croiḋe Éamuinn,
Aċt cé leor a luinne ḋe,
Is guinne an ceol 'na an croiḋe.

Ionṁuin ráib ḋo raiḋ an ċruiṫ,
Croiḋe úr, aigneaḋ oirḋearc,
Géag ṡaor raiṫréimneaċ rasaċ,
Caoṁ caiṫréimeaċ ceannasaċ.

Mór an séan ḋá ġruaiḋ ġlantais,
Buaine blaiḋ a ṫaḃartais,
Mairfiḋ beo mar ḃeirear soin,
Go ḋeo is go ḋeireaḋ ḋoṁain.

San uain ḋteirc-se ṫarla ann
Uaigneaċ an obair ḋ'Éamonn,
An caiṫleoġán go gcrú nḋil,
Aiṫbeoḋaḋ clú a ċiniḋ.

[cıan: an age, a long time; spreaʒaım: I admonish, incite, stimulate; caoṁ: gentle, mild; calm: calm; ꝼıonn: white, fair, pure, blessed, fine, pleasant; céaꝺal: singing; séıs: skill, music, voice, sigh.]It was she that could be heard a long time ago/ Encouraging the spirit of Saul/ (She was) in gentle, calm-headed, fair form/: singing psalms, free, sweet-voiced.

[coʀ: plight; aʀmacaċ: tender, careful; aꝺb: instrument; ꝺʀeaċ: countenance; ʒaoɾꝺealta: Gaelic (in the sense of natural); ꝺealb: form.] An age since the hard plight of Dolbh and Sanbh/ The tender lady (i.e. the harp), the great instrument/ (Her) countenance (is) not dark, natural, pure/ (There is) an air of magic (in) her appearance.

[ɱonʒán: a king of Ulster; ꝺaʒꝺa: the " Good God", Gaelic god of the earth, next in importance to Ꞑuaꝺa, the war-god (Gaelic Zeus or Jupiter), the mother of both (and of all the other gods) being ꝺanu, after whom the Tuatha Dé Dannan, or fairy people, are named; ʒeas: magical spell; caoıl-ꝼéaʒsaın: looking narrowly or closely; meoʀ: = méaʀ?; éascaıꝺ: nimble; cubʀaċ: foaming, frothing; cuṁʀa: fragrant, sweet.] Mongán and the son of the Daghdha/ A pair (full of) magic spells and learning/ Closely watching this music/ (Being played) by fragrant, pleasingly nimble fingers.

[ꝺíol: worth; néaṁꝺa: heavenly, divine; Ꞑıoclás ꝺall: Nick Pierce, a famous harper; conċlann: equal, rival, companion, comparison; ɾoıʀ: certainly, indeed; ıs annsa lıom: I prefer; annsa: (adjective) difficult; annsa: (noun) love; oıʀꝼꝺeaċ: musician.] Worthy of the heavenly (lady, instrument) is Blind Nicholas/ And worthy is the harp, a match/ Of the blind man to her, indeed/ And she is the love of the musician.

[conċlann: comparison; oll: great, splendid, big-hearted; loınne: joy, gladness, rapture; ʒann: scarce, narrow, restricted, limited.] (To put) anything in comparison with her powerful music/ Is not proper, – except the heart (generosity) of Eamonn/ But though the rapture of it is plenteous/ The music is less than the heart.

[ıonṁuın: dear; ráıb: a strong, generous person, hero, scion; raꝺaım: I give, furnish; oıʀꝺeaʀc: illustrious, noble; ʒéaʒ: limb, member, scion; saoʀ: free, noble, generous; raıċréımeaċ: fortunate; rasaċ: mature, vigorous; caıċréımeaċ: triumphant; ceannasaċ: powerful, commanding.] Dear (to me) the hero who handed over the harp/ A pure heart, a noble mind/ A noble, fortunate, vigorous lad/ Kind, triumphant, commanding.

[séan: good luck, success, prosperity; blaꝺ: renown; tabaʀtas: bestowing, gift.] Great the happiness to his cool fresh cheek/ Enduring the fame of his gift/ He will live greatly as this (story) is told/ Forever, and to the end of the world.

[uaın: time; teaʀc: scarce, scant, stunted; caıċ-leoʒan: lion of battle; crú: blood; ꝺıl: beloved, loyal.] In the hard time now happening/ Lonely is the work for Eamonn/ – the champion of true blood – / To revive the fame of his race.

47

Ar dteaċt ó Maiġ Luirg i le,
Fuair ollaṁnaċt is uaisle,
Is mar do ḟill an uairse ói,
Do ċinn ar uaisle aisti.

Fear naċ ceann-ċas, clú naċ gann,
Eascara an ionnṁuis Éamonn
Barr gaċ aoin an uairse do
Do ċaoiḃ uaisle is anma.

M'ionṁaine mo ċréan tobaiġ,
Meig óg inġean Conċubair,
M'annsa clí séad-rang a sreaċ
'Sí do ċéad-bronn an ċláirseaċ.

Ní baosrað, ní blað bréige,
Áille is oirbeart Mairgréige,
A haonloċt, maorðaċt, is mað,
Aobðaċt daonnaċt is deallrað.

5. **Ní maiċ uaigneas don annsa**

(Do Risteard Ua Husae.)

Ní maiċ uaigneas don annsa,
Atá a heolas agamsa,
Do ṁúin danɓa flaiċ re fios
Naċ maiċ don annsa uaigneas.

Re cúig bliaðnaib uaigneaċ inn
Gan aṁarc an ḟir álainn,
Oile taoḃ-ḟuar mar Ġoill ġlain,
Aċt aon-uair ċoir an treall soin.

Fear an toil mar sain sonn
Atá a airðeana agam
'Ɓé do ċreaċóċað a ċorp
Do ḃeaċóċað é a aṁarc.

[ı Le: = ı Leıċ, in this direction; cınnım: I progress, surpass, exceed, excel.] On coming here from Magh Luirg/ He achieved learning and nobility/ And as he now returns/ He surpasses (all) in nobility.

[ceann-ċas: "twisted head", malicious; eascara: enemy; ıonnṁas: wealth, riches (*perhaps* selfishness *here*?); barr: top, superiority.] A man (who is) not malicious, of renown not rare/ The enemy of greed (is) Eamonn/ The superior of everyone at this time/ In regard to nobility and spirit.

[ıonṁaıne: love; cRéan: = cReon, hero?; cRıan: a third; cobaım: I levy; cobaċ: act of levying; cóbacc = cábacc, importance; annsa: love; clí: body; séaö: jewel; Rang: rank, rung of a ladder; sReaċ: series, perhaps line of descent.] My love, my levied third (?= *choice*?)/ Young Meg, daughter of Conor/ Love of my breast, most valuable member of her line/ It was she who first presented the harp.

[baosRaö: folly, vanity, madness, boasting; blaö: fame; oıRbeaRc: good deed, generosity; máö: trump, fortune; maö: *perhaps* maıċ, goodness; aoböaċ: pleasant, delightful; öaonnaċc: humanity, kindness; öeallRaö: öeallRaṁ, appearance, brightness, splendour.] It is not vanity, nor false reputation/ The beauty and generosity of Margaret/ Her only fault: majesty and goodness/ (Her) charm, humanity and grandeur.

5. Solitude Is Not Good For Love

(To Richard Hussey.)

[uaıgneas: loneliness, solitude; annsa: love, friendship, affection; ḟlaıċ: lord, person of rank, gentleman.] Solitude is not good for friendship/ I have knowledge of it (*friendship*)/ A knowledgeable gentleman taught me/ That loneliness is not good for love.

[ınn: = sınn, mé, I; bıle: sacred tree, *figuratively*: scion, man of distinction; caob-ḟuaR: (literally cool-bodied), brave, healthy; goll: Goll Mac Mórna, a chief of the Fenian band; cReall: turn, while, spell.] For five years I was lonely/ Without sight of the fine man/ – A fine fellow, brave, like pure Goll – / Just once (I saw him), to the east, on that occasion.

[coıl: will, goodwill; sonn: ansonn, here; aıRöe: quality, mark, characteristic.] A man of such goodwill here/ I have the marks of it/ Whoever should destroy his (own) body/ The sight of him (Richard) would cure.

A mná uaisle, an iongnaḋ liḃ
Naċ bean Rom-meall uair éigin,
A stuaḋ ġeal gan ḟeirg gan an,
Aċt fear gan ċeilg ḋom ċealgaḋ?

Ḋá mbaḋ aiċniḋ ḋaoiḃse a ḋáil,
Tréiṫe ionganta an ógáin,
Ní biaḋ siḃ gan suirġe ris,
Mil a ḟuiġle re n-aiṫris.

Scoṫ ógán caoṁ-inse Cé
Ristearḋ Rann-ġasta husae;
Cneas so-ġealta ré ḋár reaċt,
Ḋo-leanta é i n-aintleaċt.

Lán beoil tíorṫa, tobar fis,
Ḋoras eoil airgṫeaċ ḋoilġis,
Ár gcuiḋ-ne, i bḟóḋán na bḟionn
Oiḋe ógán na hÉireann.

Óirċóir glan-ḋán ngasta ngrinn,
Uġḋar ait, ollaṁ innill,
Fear ḋaor-ḋuan bḟriṫir i bḟor
Aol-ġruaḋ go gcriṫir cearḋcán.

6. Ionṁuin t'aiseag, a Eoġain

(Ḋ'Eoin Ua Callanáin an liaiġ)

Ionṁuin t'aiseag, a Eoġain,
Moċean ḋ'ḟior an ġlé-eolais,
Tóg fám ċroiḋe brioċt loinne
Ón rioċt i raḃamair-ne.

Ní mé aṁáin ḋo ḃí mar sain,
Iomḋa ó clos t'éaga, a Eoġain,
Trom sluaġ imṡníoṁaċ i n-airc
A stuaḋ il-ġníoṁaċ orḋairc.

[meaʟʟ: entice, beguile, allure; ʀom-meaʟʟ: = ᴅo mo ṁeaʟʟaᴅ, beguiling me; scuaᴅ: curve, arch, handsome person (*figurative*); ᴀn = on, stain, fault, reproach; ceaʟᵹ: deceit; ceaʟᵹaim: I seduce, allure, amuse.] Noble women, is it a surprise to you/ That it was not a woman who beguiled me at some time?/: O bright and handsome man, without anger, without reproach:/ But a man without deceit who allured me?

[ᴅáiʟ: act of pouring out or distributing, conferring, meeting, story, legend; suiʀᵹe: wooing, love-making; ᵱuiᵹeaʟʟ: word, decision, decree; ᵱuiᵹʟe: speech, words.] If you knew his nature/ The wondrous qualities of the young man/ You would not be without courting him/ The honey of his words to be told.

[scoc: top, summit, best; caoṁ: gentle, beautiful; Inis Cé: *in Erris, County Mayo, according to Dineen, but more likely to be* Inis Cé *near Valencia*; ʀᴀnn: verse; so-ᵹeaʟca: easily whitened, fair; ʀé: moon, month, period (*fig.*) distinguished person; ʀeᴀcc: law, power, right, (*also* activity, vigour, commotion); ʀᴀcc: passion, outburst; ᴅo-leᴀnca: impossible to follow or match.] The finest of youths, from beautiful Inis Cé/ Richard Hussey of clever verses/ Bright-featured light of our dispensation(?)/ Incomparable in intellect.

[Lán beoiʟ: the full of the mouth, the whole talk; ᴀiʀᵹceaċ: plunderer; ᴅoilᵹeas: melancholy, affliction, torment; cuᴅo: share, meal, property, *also term of endearment*; ᵱóᴅán nᴀ bᵱionn: *fig. for Ireland*.] The whole (subject of) talk of countries, well of knowledge/ Doorway to learning, destroyer of grief/ Our darling, in the Land of the Fair/ The teacher of the youth of Ireland.

[óʀcóiʀ: person who gilds, embellisher; ᵹlán: clean, full, exact; ᴀic: pleasant, droll; innilʟ: safe, secure, ready; ᴅaoʀ: dear, expensive; ᵱʀiciʀ: eager,earnest; ᵱoʀ: ?*Dineen suggest this may a class of metre in* ᴅán ᴅíʀeaċ; ᵱúʀ: preparation; cʀiciʀ: spark.] Embellisher of well-made poems (which are) clever (and) humorous/ Pleasing author, sure authority/ Man of valuable poems, industrious in their preparation/ White-cheeked until (reddened by) the spark of the forge (of composition).

6. I Am Glad Of Your Recovery, Eoin

(For Eoin O'Callanan, the physician)

[ionṁuin: dear, beloved; ᴀiseaᵹ: recovery (from illness); moceᴀn: greetings, my regards; ᵹlé: clear, perfect, manifest; bʀiocc: charm, incantation; loinn: joy, rapture.] I am happy for your recovery, Eoin/ My regards to the man of (who brought) true knowledge (of your recovery)/ (And who) gave to my heart a magic spell of rapture/ From the state in which we were (before).

[cʀom sluaᵹ: large number; imsníoṁáċ: worried; ᴀiʀc: greed, great hunger, want, hardship; scuaᴅ: arch, support, champion; oiʀᴅeᴀʀc: splendid, illustrious, noble.] I was not the only person who was like that/ Many, from the time they heard (a report) of your death, Eoin/ – a great crowd worried, in despair/ O noble champion of great deeds.

51

Glóir 'na díol do Dia Aċar
Beiċ duiċ-se gan deonaċaḋ,
A réalċ eoil, gan ċeilċ, gan ċuir,
Is gan deoir rem ḋeirc iċ ḋeaġaiḋ.

Níor b'ionann aoinneaċ oile
Is ċusa daṁ-sa, a ḋeaġ-ruire,
Ḟuaimenċ oile níor ṁeall mé,
Is ḟearr duine 'ná daoine.

Do bíċeá daṁsa, a ḋreaċ nár,
Iċ cóṁairleaċ, iċ ċompán,
Iċ bráċair ḟeile im ḟail,
'S i dċráċaib eile iċ aċair.

Muna mbeinn dod ċléib cleaċċa,
Mar ċáim, a ḟéil inċleaċċa
A ṡlaċ 's a ṡeise dom ċoil
Mise níor ṁac dom aċair.

Ní ḟaca aoinneaċ ċusa
'S níor éisċ bós do briaċra-sa
Nár liġ do ċás 'na ċás air,
'S dar lib do bás a bás-soin.

Is gearr geaṁ-oiḋċe iċ ḟoċair,
Céarna ċreabluid ċionnscadail,
Is gan láṁ do ċur óm ċuim,
Naċ am i ngliaiḋ ná i n-iorġuil.

Ḟairsing ċ'eolas a ġairċ-ṁic,
O Arcċic go hAnċairċċic,
'S ó aibéis go laoi ċréan duiċ
Ḟad ḟis a n-airgne agaċ.

Agaċ do ġéabċaoi, a ġruaiḋ ċe,
Ceirċ-breiċ cille is ċuaiċe,
Cosc do ġráḋ caoi gaċ uilc,
Daṁna dearg-láṁ do ḋíogáilċ.

52

[oíol: due share, reqital, retribution; ᵭeonᴀᴄᴀᵭ: hurt, injury; ceiʟᴄ: concealment; cuʀ: authority, jurisdiction; ᵭeᴀʀc: eye; ᵭeᴀᵹᴀɪᵭ: ᵭɪᴀɪᵭ.] Glory to God the Father in recompense for/ You being without harm/ O star of learning, without concealment, without superior/ And without (me having to have) a tear in my eye after you.

[ʀuɪʀe: over-king, knight, lord; ꜰuᴀɪmenᴄ: foundation, vigour, sense; oɪʟe: eɪʟe or uɪʟe?] Nobody else was the same/ As you (are) to me, O good knight/ The mass of all (others) did not attract me/ A (single) person is greater than (the totality of) people.

[ᵭʀeᴀᴄ: countenance; nᴀ́ʀ: (shameful, ashamed), modest, honourable, noble; ꜰeiʟe?: (ꜰeiʟim: I suit, ꜰeiʟiúnᴀᴄ: suitable; ꜰiʟe: poet; ꜰuiʟ: blood, kin); ꜰᴀiʟ: resting place, bed, couch.] You were to me, O noble countenance/ An adviser, a companion/ A brother of (my own) blood in my refuge/ And at other times a father (to me).

[cʟeᴀᴄᴄ: habit, custom; cʟéiᵬ-cʟeᴀᴄᴄ: bosom companionship; sʟᴀᴄ: (rod, rib, staff, wand), youth, prince, chief; seise: companion, favourite; ᵭom ᴄoiʟ: to my liking.] Were I not one of your bosom companions/ As I am, O generous, intellectual (person)/ O prince and O favourite companion/ I would not be a son to my father.

[ᵬós: ꜰós, yet, besides, also; ʟuiᵹim: I lie down, encroach upon; cᴀ́s: cause, case difficulty.] Nobody (ever) saw you/ And listened, besides, to your words/ That your cause did not become his cause/ And, it would seem to you, your death (was) his death.

[ᵹeᴀṁ-oɪᵭce: winter's night; céᴀʀnᴀ: recovery; ᴄʀeᴀᵬʟuɪᵭ: trouble; ᴄɪonnscᴀᵭᴀʟ: labour, work, undertaking; com: waist; ᵹᴀn ʟᴀ́ṁ ᵭo ᴄuʀ óm ᴄuim: *Dineen interprets this as "holding my sides (with laughter)"*; nᴀᴄ: any, every (= ᵹᴀᴄ); ᵹʟiᴀᵭ: battle; ɪoʀᵹᴀiʟ: attack, battle-field.] A winter's night is short in your company/ (You are the) relief from the trouble of hard work/ And without taking a hand from my waist/ Every time of battle and attack..

[ᵹᴀʀᴄ: cheerful, clever, noble, generous; ᴀiᵬéis: drollery, exaggeration, nonsense; ʟᴀoɪ: lay, poem; ᴄʀéᴀn: powerful, intense, expert; ꜰᴀᵭ ꜰis: fullness of knowledge; ᴀɪʀᵹneᴀᴄ: peevish, angry.] Wide your knowledge, O clever youth/ From the Arctic to the Antarctic/ And from light verse to serious poetry/ You have full knowledge of the pains (of composition).

[ᵬʀeiᴄ: judgement; ciʟʟ: church, ᴄuᴀᴄ: northern, sinister, of the common people; cosc: restraint, hindrance; cᴀoɪ: road, condition, circumstances; ᵭᴀṁnᴀ: matter, material, cause, motive; ᵭeᴀʀᵹ-ʟᴀ́ṁ: red (*or* bloody) hand, wrong-doing; ᵭíoᵹᴀʟᴄᴀs: vengeance.] From you is to be obtained, O warm cheek/ The correct judgement of sacred and profane/ The restriction of love, the circumstances of evil/ The grounds for vengeance on hand of blood.

Ʒé mbaö ꝺoċtúir ʒaċ ꝺuine
Ꝺá ḃꝼuil i n-iaṫ luʒuine,
Is tú ꝺo ꝼreaʒra, a ślaṫ śuilt,
Leaṫ a heaʒna 's a haöuint.

Óṫ órꝺ ꝼéin ar ꝼeaö Ḃanḃa,
Cóir ꝼuarais céim caṫarꝺa,
Ḃarr ar anóir ʒaċ ꝼisiʒ
Ó anꝺóiʒ 's ó öeiʒ-ꝼisiḃ.

Ó ꝺo ṫárla-sa taoḃ riot,
Mo ċráö-sa cráö na ʒcaraꝺ,
A ḃeoil ꝼairsinʒ is ꝺom ꝼuil,
A Eoʒain, t'aiseaʒ is ionṁuin.

7. Má's é an leoʒan cróöa Ʒaeöeal

(Ar Eoʒan Ruaö Ua Néill)

Má's é an leoʒan cróöa Ʒaeöeal i ʒceart
Ꝺo ḃéarꝼas ꝼóꝺ ʒlan Ꝼóꝺla ꝼé n-a smaċt,
A ḃꝼaice-se, a stóċaiʒ ċróin noċ téꝺ tar lear,
Ꝺeir cum Eoʒain móir Uí Néill an ʒlac.

Donnċaö Maol Ua Súilleaḃáin aʒ ꝼreaʒra:

Tuʒais uait an ʒlac ʒo léir
Tar ceart, a Ṗiarais ꝼeiritéir,
Ó ainṁire śleaċta Éiḃir Ꝼinn
Ainḃꝼios teaċta ꝺot ċéaꝺ-rinn.

8. Nuair naċ ꝼéiꝺir cur ret ċeirꝺ

(Aʒ ꝼreaʒra ar ḃárꝺ ꝺar b'ainm Ristearꝺ)

Nuair naċ ꝼéiꝺir cur ret ċeirꝺ,
Ná bualaö roiṁe, a Risteirꝺ,
Mar is uaim ór is uṁa
Éiʒse Ꝼóꝺla t'ꝼoʒluʒa.

[ιλċ: field; λλċ luₛλιne: *figurative for Ireland*; ϝReλₛRλιm: I answer, answer favourably, suit, correspond to; sλλċ: rod, youth, chief; suλċ: merriment, best; eλₛnλ: science, knowledge; λὒnλὒ: kindling, inflaming, illuminating.] Even though everyone were a doctor/ That is in the field of Iughain/ It is you that answers, you merry fellow/ Yours is the science and illumination (of Ireland).

[óRὒ: order, caste, kind; cóιR: right, true; céιm: degree, grade, rank; cλċλRὒλ: civic; ϝιseλċ: physician; λnὒóιₛ: unlikely one, one from whom something is not expected, lowly person; ὒειₛ-ϝιs: *from* ϝιos, knowledge.] From your own kind in the whole of Ireland/ You rightly obtained civic rank/ Excelling in honour every physician/ From the unlikely to the knowledgable.

[cλoὒ Rιoċ: close to you (in kinship); beoλ ϝλιRsιnₛ: "wide mouth", open, well-spoken person; λιseλₛ: recovery; ιonṁuιn: dear, happy.] As I happen to be close to you (in kinship)/ My torment was the torment of *(felt by)* relatives/ O person of kind words who is of my blood/ O Eoin, I am happy for your recovery.

7. If It Is The Brave Lion Of The Irish

(On Owen Roe O'Neill)

[ϝóὒ: sod, land; ϝλιc: jot, nothing; λ ὒϝλιce-se: *In the 1903 edition, Dineen interprets this as* ι ὒϝλιce-sι *(in this scrap (of poetry or paper)), while in the 1934 edition he interprets it as* cλὒλιR λιRe, *or* ϝéλċ *(Look here!);* scócλċ: a tall pole, the mast of a ship; cRón: tan, copper-coloured,brown, dark red; ₛλλc: fist, grasp, power, authority.] If it is the brave lion of the Irish truly/ Who shall take the whole land of Ireland under his control/ In this scrap (of verse), O brown mast who is going overseas/ Take to great Owen O'Neill the authority.

Bald Donnchadh O'Sullivan Answering:

[meλR: swift; mire: rapidity, ardour; λιṁιRe: great ardour?; sλιoċc: people; sλιoċc ÉιὒιR ϝιnn: *the people of Munster?*; Note: *the prefix* λn- *sometimes denotes intensification, sometimes negation; in any case, O'Sullivan's reply seems to be a rejection of command being given to an Ulsterman;* λιnὒϝιos: ignorance; ceλċcλ: message; céλὒ-Rιnn: *a kind of metre in* ὒλn ὒíReλċ, *hence verse.*] You gave away the whole authority/ – Beyond what was right, O Pierce Ferriter – / From the ardour of the people of Éibhear Fionn/ An ignorant message (is) your verse.

Note: *Owen Roe arrived in Ireland in July 1642 to lead the armies of the Confederation.*

8. When You Cannot Add To Your Craft

(Replying to a bard named Richard)

[CuιRιm λe: I add to, improve; buλιλιm: I proceed; uλιm: joining together; uṁλ: bronze, brass; ϝoₛλuₛλὒ: plundering, laying waste.] If you cannot improve your art/ Do not carry on with it, Richard/ For it is the mixing of gold and brass/ To destroy the poetry of Ireland. [uλιm *also means alliteration, and since the words* óR *and* uṁλ *are not in perfect alliteration, the third line can also be reference to technical faults in the work of the poet who is being criticised. Interpreted this way, the line would read:* mλR ιs uλιm "óR" ιs "uṁλ". *The fact that the nouns are in their nominative rather than genitive forms supports this interpretation.*]

Cruiṫneaċt is coġal aṁlaið,
Fiú an t-oiðeas fuaramair,
Mo ṡaoṫ-sa, 'aṫḟlaiṫ ċar ṫoil,
Mé iṫ árus iṫ ḟiaċaib.

E. Mac Ġ. cct. aġ freaġra.

Dá mb'ḟéiðir ʒo mbéaraið ar Piaras bárr
Aoinne ar aonċor i n-iaċaib Fáil
Cum ðaor-ḃruiðe réiðteaċ is riarċa ar ðáiṁ
'Sé Éamonn an té seo anois ċiar i n-'áiṫ.

9. Cuʒas annsaċt ð'óiʒ Ġallða

(Do Ṁeiʒ Ruiséil)

Cuʒas annsaċt ð'óiʒ Ġallða,
Inʒean ċruṫ-ġlan ċéimbanða,
Scuaið ollġaoṫ ʒan ḟuaṫ ʒan oil,
D'uaṫ na lonnlaoċ ó Lonðain.

Cuʒas: nárab misce me,
Nárab mó is misce ise:
Searc m'anma ð'inʒin an Ġaill
Don ḟinn-ġil aṁra álainn.

An croiðe ʒan ceað ðaṁsa
A raib ð'annsa ionnamsa,
Cuʒ uaim ʒo nʒeilt-ċuinʒ nʒusa,
Don scuaið nʒeilṫruim nĠallða-so.

Aoinḃean eile ní ḃfuiʒḃeað
A n-uair uaim an Lonðain-ḃean,
Ní hé aṁáin is ðoiliʒ ðaṁ,
Ġráð ðom oiʒið 's ðom aðnað.

Ionʒnað naċ ionṁaoiðim ðaṁ
Ʒo meallann is naċ meallṫar
Bean mé ðo aiṫ-ċreaċ oram
Naċ clé aiṫreaċ uraʒall.

56

[coʒᴀl: corn-cockle, weed; sᴀoċ: distress, punishment; ᴀ́ʀus: house; 'ᴀċḟlᴀiċ: ᴀ ḟlᴀiċ?; iċ ḟiᴀċᴀib: in your debt.] (As) wheat and cockle likewise/ (Was) even the instruction we *(you and I?)* got/ It is my distress, Sir, by your leave/ That I (was ever) in your house (thus becoming) indebted to you.

E. Mac G. Composed *(the following)* **In Reply.**

If it is possible that (anyone) could surpass Pierce/ Anyone at all in the lands of Ireland/ In solving and settling the severe quarrels of poets/ It is Eamonn (who is) such a one now back there in his place. (*Dineen suggests that the Eamonn referred to was Pierce's father, or another relative.*)

9. I Gave Love To A Foreign Maiden

(To Meg Russell)

[Meg Russell was related to William Russell (1558-1613) who was a royal official sent to Ireland.]

[ᴀnnsᴀċċ: love; óiʒ: maid, virgin; inʒeᴀn: daughter, girl; céimbᴀnoᴀ: of feminine step or gait; scuᴀ́ò: arch, princess; ʒᴀoċ: subtle, prudent; ḟuᴀċ: hate, enmity; oil: reproach, scandal; uᴀċ: ?*adjective meaning* lonely?; uᴀ: grandchild, descendant; lonn: strong, brave, fierce.] I gave (my) love to a foreign maiden/ A girl of neat form and feminine gait/ A very prudent princess, without enmity, without reproach/ Of the breed of the brave warriors from London.

[ní misce mé: I am not worse for (something); ní mó nᴀ́: no more than; seᴀʀc: (sexual) love; ᴀṁʀᴀ: great, noble, wonderful.] I gave: and I was none the worse (for it)/ No more than she was any the worse (for it): / The love of my soul to the daughter of the foreigner/ To the fair, bright (girl), wonderful, beautiful.

[ʒeᴀlc: madman; cuinʒ: bond, promise; ʒusᴀ: strong feelings, desires; ʒeilcʀuim: ?; ʒeᴀl-cʀom?: *Dineen suggests* fair and sedate.] The heart, without my permission,/ What there was of love in me,/ Gave (it) from me with passions (of) reckless commitment/ To this princess (of the sedate?) foreigners.

[ᴀ n-uᴀiʀ: *the 1903 edition has* ᴀ bḟuᴀiʀ (what was obtained); ooiliʒ: grievous, troublesome; oiʒʀò: act of killing or destroying; ᴀònᴀim: kindle, inflame, burn.] Any other woman would not get/ What this London-woman received from me/ Not this only is troubling me/ (But also) love is destroying and consuming me.

[mᴀoròim oo: I "cast up" to or against; meᴀllᴀim: I entice, seduce; clé: left-handed, awkward; ᴀiċreᴀċ: sorry, troubled; ᴀċᴀʀʀᴀċ: a change, transformation; uʀᴀ̊ʒᴀll: ?; uʀċᴀll: spancel, fetter, shackle, predicament.] It is a wonder that it is not strongly cast up to me/ That – allures but is not allured by – / A woman (*allures but is not allured by:* (*from the previous line*)) me, (a woman) who defeated me utterly/ (– Me who) am not awkward (in any) other predicament!

Meiġ Ruséil Ríoġan Ġallḋa,
Réalta śuaiṫniḋ śaorċlannḋa,
Uḃall óir is cian rom-ċar,
Ġrian aġus ġlóir na nĠallḃan.

Ḋo-ní a ḟolt ór ḋ'uṁa
Is san ló a rosc réilteanna,
Croiḋe uar na n-airġiall ḋte,
'S a ġruaḋ ainġrian ast-oiḋċe.

Ḋuḃaiḋ a cneas an ġéis ġeal,
'S a ḋá cóirḋearc an cristeal,
Tuġ fionna ar an rós reiṁe,
Ionġa is ós na hinġeine.

Caoiniḋ a aimsir uaiṫe aġ ḋul,
Anṁain naċ féaḋ 'na foċair,
Is ġaċ bionnśruṫ suas le sin,
Ḋiomḋaċ ḋo luas an leanḃsoin.

Mar a mbíḋ is breaċ ḋaṁsa,
Lá i n-oiḋċe san ionaḋso,
'S ġaċ lá ḋoilḃċe naċ só soin,
Is oiḋċe san ló an lá soin.

Ainnear onġta an óiġ ġan ċuir,
Aon uair mar a mbí bliaḋain,
Rún ciallaiḋ ġan uaill ġan oil,
Bliaḋain uair aċt 'na hoċair.

Ó n-a croḃ cuṁra ġaċ crann,
Mil mar ġlacas an ġrafann,
'S ḋá mbeana ris rós roḋ-ḟear
A hós ar ḋris 's ar ḋraiġean.

Ḋá ḃfaiceaḋ neaċ, neaṁ-nár ḋi,
Ise 's an ġrian san ġeiṁre,
Ann féin 's i nġaċ aon eile
Ḋá ġréin iaḋ i n-aon-roiḋe.

[ʀíoᵹᴀɪn: noblewoman; sᴜᴀɪⵜⵏⵔö: well-known, notable, illustrious; sᴀoʀ: free, noble; sᴀoʀ-ⵜLᴀⵏⵏⵟᴏᴀ: of noble stock.] Meg Russell, foreign noblewoman/ Illustrious, high-born star/ Apple of gold, long loved by me/ The sun and glory of the foreign women.

[ᵱoLⵜ: hair, tresses; ᴜⵎᴀ: copper; ʀosⵜ: eye; ⵜʀoⵔöe: heart, love, affection; ᴜᴀʀ: ? ᵱᴜᴀʀᴀɪm: I cool, relieve; ᴀʀᵹᴀL: contention, confusion; ᴀɪⵏᵹʀɪᴀⵏ: a bright sun.] Her tresses would make gold of copper/ And in day(light) her eyes (become) stars/ Her affection cools heated contention/ And her cheek is a bright sun by night.

[ᵹéɪs: swan; ⵟeᴀʀⵜ: eye; ⵜóɪʀ-ⵟeᴀʀⵜ: true eye; ᵱɪoⵏⵏᴀ: speck, paling (in comparison with); ɪoⵏᵹᴀ: fingernail; ós: mouth.] Her skin would darken the white swan (by comparison)/ And her two true eyes (would darken) crystal/ The rose pales before her/ The nail and mouth of the girl.

[ᴀɪmseᴀʀ: time, season; ᴀⵏⵎᴀɪⵏ: ᵱᴀⵏᴀⵎᴀɪⵏ: to remain; ᵱéᴀⵟᴀɪm: I am able; ᵱoⵜᴀɪʀ: company; ⵟɪoⵎⵟᴀⵜ: disappointed, envious; Lᴜᴀs: speed; Leᴀⵏⵟ: child, dear one, fair lady.] Her seasons lament their departing from her/ That they are unable to stay with her/ And every sweet stream (giving) up (*way*) to her/ Envious of the swiftness of the dear one.

[ⵟʀeᴀⵜ: judgement, opinion; Lᴀ ɪ n-oⵔöⵜe: *?should be* Lᴀ ᴀn oɪöⵜe?; ɪoⵏᴀⵟ: place; ⵟoɪLⵟⵜe: mysterious, sad; sóᵹ: joy, ease; sóᵹᴀⵜ: happy, comfortable.] Where she is, in my opinion/ The night is day in that place/ And every sad day that I am deprived (of her)/ It is night by day on such a day.

[ᴀɪⵏⵏeᴀʀ: maiden; oⵏᵹᴀɪm: I daub, anoint, hallow; óɪᵹ: virgin; ⵜoʀ: a throw, a move, a trick; ʀúⵏ: sweetheart; ⵜɪᴀLLᴀⵔö: sensible?; ᴜᴀɪLL: vanity; oɪL: stain, reproach.] A hallowed maiden (is) the virgin without deceit/ A year (is like) an hour where (ever) she (happens to) be/ Sensible sweetheart, without vanity, without fault/ An hour is a year unless it is in her company.

[ⵜʀoⵟ: claw, hand; ⵜᴜⵎʀᴀ: fragrant; mɪL: honey; ᵹᴀᵱᴀⵏⵏ: henbane; beᴀⵏᴀɪm: I strike, touch; ᵱeᴀʀᴀɪm: I give forth, multiply; ós: mouth; ⵟʀɪs: driseog, thorn, bramble, briar; ⵟʀᴀɪᵹeᴀⵏ: a blackthorn.] From her touch every tree (becomes) fragrant/ Honey (springs forth) as she handles the henbane / And if a rose touches her, it gives forth (*bears fruit?*)/ Her lips (=*gentle touch?*) on briar and blackthorn (*the thornbushes become smooth to touch?*).

[neᴀⵜ: a being, anyone; nᴀʀ: ashamed; neᴀⵎ-nᴀʀ: opposite of ashamed; ʀoɪⵜɪm: I arrive.] If anyone saw her, – no shame to her – / She is the sun in winter/ To that person, and to everyone else/ (She is like) two suns that are come together.

Nár ba hiomcur d'ḟiaċ a corp,
Dá mbuḋ eaḋ dob ḟiaċ éaḋroċt,
Is cloċ ġairt dá bḟéaġaḋ ḟair,
Go ndéanaḋ cailc don ċloċ soin.

Atá ní ḟá n-a ḟearta
Fuil Ġallda gníoṁ Ġaeḋealda,
Is Ġall-ġníoṁ an méd is maċ,
I ngéig ṡalm-ṡaoir na saltraċ.

Siúr Iarla Essex ḟuair uilc,
Is diuic díċeannta an ór-ḟuilt,
Luċt suġ-ċorp is ngairt-ṗort ngnaoi
Hairḟort Suḟolc is Suraoi.

Maiċ ḋó a ġaol 'na goire
Iarla calma Ċorcaiġe,
'S do ġrianġa na gcealgċolg gcuir
D'Iarla Deadford a bráċair.

Uilliam Ruiséil ruire seang,
Ġiúistís oirḋearc na hÉireann,
Noċar taom timḋiḃe ḋi
Ġaol an ḟinn-ḃile innti.

Ní do ċairgeas dom ḋeoin di,
Níor ġlac is do ġoid an nísin;
Iongnaḋ an tsloid dá saoirlí sonn,
Aoinní de ġoid ní ġlacann.

Ní ḟeaca mé don tsaoir séiṁ
Adciú, a Ċaitilín Ruiséil,
Ní rug glionn-Ḃanḃa a geall so,
Ceann is ionlaḃra aċt tusa.

[ᚱᴉᴀċ: debt, fine, duty; éᴀᴏᴦᴏċᴄ: bright, brilliant, clear, manifest; ᴣᴀᴉᴦᴄ: strong? *Dineen suggests* ᴣᴀᴦb, rough; cloċ ᴣoᴉᴦᴄ: field stone; ᴏᴀ́ bᴦéᴀᴣᴀᴏ ᴦᴀᴉᴦ: ᴏᴀ́ bᴦéᴀċᴀᴏ sí ᴀᴉᴦ.] Her person did not carry debt/ (But) if it were so, it would be an honourable debt(?)/ And if (she) were to look upon a hard rock/ The rock would become (as soft as) chalk.

[ᴠí: a thing; ᴦeᴀᴦᴄ: virtue, power; ᴣᴠíoᴍ: deed, action; ᴍᴀċ: ᴍᴀᴉċ; ᴣéᴀᴣ: young person, scion; sᴀʟm: psalm; sᴀʟm-sᴀᴏᴉᴦ: unrestrained in psalms, (*the 1903 edition has* sᴀʟm-síoᴦ: continually psalm(-singing)); sᴀʟᴄᴀᴉᴦ (*genitive* sᴀʟᴄᴦᴀċ): psalter, book of psalms or poems.] There is something (special) under(-lying) her virtue/ Foreign blood, Irish deeds (*behaviour*)/ And (also) foreign deeds: just those which are good:/ In the scion of the hymnbook, unrestrained in psalm(-singing).

[sᴉúᴦ: sister, female relative; ᴏíceᴀnnᴄᴀ: beheaded; súᴣ: juice, secretion; súᴣᴀċ: merry; sóᴣ: joy, ease; so-: *prefix denoting positivity and feasibility*; ᴣᴀᴉᴦᴄ-ᴘoᴦᴄ: strong mansion *or* fort; ᴣnᴀoᴉ: pleasant, delightful.] Relative of the Earl of Essex to whom harm befell/ And of the golden-haired duke who was beheaded/ Of the people of strong bodies and strong, delightful mansions/ Of Hartford, Suffolk and Surrey.

['nᴀ ᴣoᴉᴦe: in her proximity; ʟᴀᴦʟᴀ Ċoᴦcᴀᴉᴣe: *Richard Boyle became Earl of Cork in 1620*; ᴣᴀ: dart; ᴣᴦᴉᴀnᴣᴀ: a brilliant dart, *fig. for* hero; coʟᴣ: sword, spear, point of weapon; ceᴀʟᴣcoʟᴣ: sting, plot, guile; coᴦ: throw, turn, spell; coᴦ: wearying, tiring; ʟᴀᴦʟᴀ beᴀᴏᴦoᴦᴏ: *a son of William Russell became the Earl of Bedford in 1627*; ᴀ bᴦᴀ́ᴄᴀᴉᴦ: *1903 edition has* 's ᴏᴀ́ bᴦᴀ́ᴄᴀᴉᴦ.] It is a good thing for him, his relationship to her,/ – The brave earl of Cork – / And (it is good) for the hero of victorious, guileful arms/ For the Earl of Bedford and for his brother.

[ᴦuᴉᴦe: nobleman, seᴀnᴣ: graceful, slender; oᴉᴦᴏeᴀᴦᴄ: illustrious; ᴄᴀom: fit, disease; ᴄᴉᴍᴏ̀ᴉbe: ruinous, destructive; bᴉʟe: champion.] William Russell, graceful nobleman/ Illustrious Justice of Ireland/ – It is not a destructive ailment to her/ That she is related to the fair champion.

[ᴀn nísᴉn: ᴀn ní sᴉn; sʟᴀᴏ: plunder; ʟí: colour, complexion, beauty; ᴣoᴏ: stealing, theft, stolen goods; ᴀoᴉnní ᴏe ᴣoᴏ: *1903 edition has* ᴀon ní ᴏᴀoᴦ.] The thing which I offered (*my affection*) of my own volition/ (She) did not accept and (yet) she stole that thing!/ (Such) plunder is surprising for that generous beauty/ Anything stolen she does not (usually) accept!

[ᴦeᴀcᴀᴉm: I bend, bow, genuflect; sᴀoᴦ: mason, architect, creator; séᴍ: fine, mild, placid, graceful; ᴀᴏ-ċᴉú: I saw; ᴣʟᴉnn: pure, clear, plain; ᴣeᴀʟʟ: likeness; ᴉonʟᴀbᴦᴀ: worthy to be spoken of; ceᴀnn ᴉs ᴉonʟᴀbᴦᴀ ᴀċᴄ ᴄusᴀ: *1903 edition has* ceᴀnnᴀs ᴉonʟᴀbᴦᴀ ᴉs ᴄusᴀ.] I did not pay homage to the fair creator (of Meg)/ I saw, Catherine Russell/ That pure Ireland did not give birth to her like!/ You are the one to be celebrated!

Léig díot t'airm, a mhacaoimh mná,
Muna fearr leat cách do lot,
Muna léigir na hairm sin díot,
Cuirfead bannaídhe d'áirighte ort.

Má chuireann tú t'airm ar gcúl,
Foiligh feasta do chúl cas,
Ná léig leis do bhrághaid bhán,
Nár léig duine do chách as.

Má shíleann tú féin, a bhean,
Nár mharbhais aon theas ná thuaidh,
Do mhairbh silleadh do shúl rín
Cách uile gan scín gan tuaigh.

Dar leat acht cé maol do ghlún,
Dar fós acht cé húr do ghlac,
Do loit gach n-aon dá bhfaca iad,
Ní fearra dhuit sciath is ga.

Foiligh orm t'ucht mar aol,
Ná feictear fós do thaobh gheal,
Ar ghrádh Críost ná feiceadh cách,
Do chíoch ró-gheal mar bhláth dos.

Foiligh orm do rosc rínn,
Má théid ar mhairbhis díob leat,
Ar ghrádh t'anma dún do bhéal,
Ná feiceadh aon do dhéad gheal.

Má's leor leat ar chuiris tím,
Sul a gcuirtear sinn i gcré,
A bhean atá reamh ró-chlaoidh,
Na hairm sin díot-sa léig.

10. Lay Down Your Arms, Young Woman

[Léiʒim: Leiʒim, I let, lay, leave, place, release; Léiʒim ʋe: I give up, abandon; mᴀcᴀoṁ: young person; cᴀ́ċ: everyone; Loicim: I destroy; bᴀnnᴀ: bond, surety; bᴀnnᴀiʋe: bail, security, guarantee.] Lay down your weapons, young woman/ Unless you prefer to destroy everyone/ If you do not lay down those weapons/ I shall impose certain sureties on you!

[ᴀʀ ʒcúl: behind, privately; ʀeᴀsᴄᴀ: from now on, therefore, so; cúl: back, back of the head, poll, head of hair, hair on the back of the head; Leiʒim Liom: I leave, concede, allow to go ahead, do not interfere with; bʀᴀ́ʒᴀiʋ: breast; Leiʒim ᴀs: I let out, extract, allow to escape, exempt, dispense from.] As you hide your weapons/ So conceal your curly hair/ Do not give give your white bosom its freedom/ That (never) allowed anyone to escape!

[siLim: I drip, shed, distil, melt, droop, hang; ʀinn: keen, piercing.] If you think, yourself, woman,/ That you did not kill anyone, south or north,/ (Well, even) the (glances) flowing from your keen eyes killed/ All, everyone, without knife or axe.

You would think, – so smooth your knees/ And too, so cool your hand/ Which destroyed everyone who saw them/ – That a shield and spear (would destroy everyone) no better for you!

[ᴄᴀoḃ: side, body; ʋos: bush, copse, tuft (of flowers).] Conceal from me your bosom like lime/ Let your fair body not be seen yet/ For the love of Christ let everyone not see/ Your too-bright breasts, like a bunch of flowers.

[ᴄéiʒim Le: I go with, bring, side with, consort with, cultivate or follow, take after or resemble.] Conceal from me your keen eyes/ If those whom you killed with them are to side with (forgive?) you/ On the love of your soul keep your mouth closed/ Let no one see your bright teeth.

[ᴀʀ ċuiʀis ᴄím: 1903 edition has ᴀʀ ċuiʀis ᴄim, which Dineen interprets as those whom you rendered powerless; cuiʀim: I bury; 'ᴄím: ? I see; ʀeᴀm ʀó-ċLᴀoiʋ: defeating me utterly.] If those you have rendered powerless are enough for you/ Before we are buried in the earth/ O woman who are defeating me utterly/ Those arms, lay them down!

Deacair teaċt ó ġalar ġráiḋ,
An galar ḋom-ċar ꝼá ċiaiċ,
Ní bí an galar gan goin bróin,
Galar naċ ꝼóir luiḃ ná liaiġ.

Galar ġráiḋ is galar ḋaṁ,
An galar go bráṫ n-ár mbun,
Im ċroiḋe ḋo ċóiḋ isteaċ,
Cneaḋ toile lér ḋóiġ mo ḋul.

Ar marṫain béaraiḋ go buan,
Ní laṁṫar céaḋtoil ḋo ċlóḋ,
Ḋo ċuir sin sin im luing-se a lán,
Ní ġráḋ cuimse linn bus lór.

Tonn seirce 'na tuile tríom,
Tuile le' mbeirṫear ar mbuaiḋ,
Tug soin ag snoiḋe go cnáṁ:
Ḋoiġ ġráiḋ im ċroiḋe ḋo ċuaiḋ.

Ní le ꝼaoḃar ġráiḋ romġoin,
Baoġal mar atáim óm ṫoil,
Ní ꝼéiḋir ḋol saor mar sin,
Niṁ mo ġon ḋon taoḃ istoiġ.

Gaoi ġráiḋ ag tollaḋ mo ṫaoiḃ,
Créaḋ ḋo b'áil ḋá ċur i gcéill
Ní ḃfuil caḃair i nḋán ḋúinn,
Mo ġráḋ rúin ḋá ḃꝼaġainn ꝼéin.

Ag so céime Ḋé na nḋúl,
Ar an té ḋá ḋtugas ġráḋ,
Troiġ ṫana 'gus seang-ḃonn saor,
Mala ċaol ḋá nḋealḃam ḋán.

Ꝼuilt ḋlúiṫe is ḋíon ar ġaċ sín
Tug an Ḋúileaṁ ḋí mar ġlóir,
Gaċ ꝼáinne cromċas ḋá céiḃ,
Ar néiṁ ꝼolċas áille an óir.

10. It Is Hard To Recover From The Fever Of Love.

[ᴄᴀᵹᴀɪm ó: I come from, recover from; ᵹᴀʟᴀʀ: disease, fever; ᴅom ċᴀʀ: ᴅom ċuʀ, putting me; ᴄɪᴀċ: oppression, hoarseness, asthma, mist; ní bí: ní bíonn; ʟuɪb: herb; ʟɪᴀɪᵹ: doctor.] It is hard to recover from the fever of love/ The fever that is smothering me/ The fever is not without wounding sorrow/ A fever that herb nor doctor cannot remedy.

[ɪ mo bun: about me, "at me"; ᴅo ċóɾ̇ò: ᴅo ċuᴀɪᵹ; cneᴀċ: cneᴀ̇ò, wound, injury; mo ̇òuʟ: my departure, death.] A fever of love is my ailment/ The ailment that is constantly upon me/ In(to) my heart it went inside/ An impairment of my will that is likely (to be the cause of) my death.

[mᴀʀċᴀɪn: living, surviving, remaining; beɪʀɪm: I bear, take, bring, bring forth, buᴀn: lasting, certain; ní ʟᴀ̇ṁċᴀʀ: ní ʟeoṁċᴀʀ, it is not allowed; céᴀᴅᴄoɪʟ: first wish; cʟó̇ʒᴀɪm: I change, alter; ᴀ ʟᴀ́n: its fullness; cuɪmse: sufficiency, moderation; bus ʟóʀ: ᴀ beᴀs ʟeoʀ, that will be sufficient.] To (all of) the living it happens for sure (?)/ It is not permitted (to anyone) to change their first choice/ That one (= *she, it?*) put in (the sails of) my ship their fullness (of wind)/ It is not a moderate love that is sufficient for us.

[ᴀ́ʀ mbuᴀɾ̇ò: my defeat; snoɾ̇òe: hewing, sculpturing; ᴅoɪᵹ: pang, stitch, dart of pain.] A wave of love flooding through me/ The flood which achieved my defeat/ It commenced chiselling me (through) to the bone/ A dart of love went into my heart.

[ᶠᴀobᴀʀ: edge, weapon; ᴄoɪʟ: will, wilfullness, choice, caprice.] It is not by a weapon, (it is by) love that I am being wounded/ The danger to me is from my (own) choice/ Therefore it is not possible to escape/ The poison of my wound is inside me.

[ᵹᴀoɪ: ᵹᴀ, dart, lance; ᴄoʟʟᴀɪm: I pierce, penetrate; ᴄᴀob: side, body; cuɪʀɪm ɪ ᵹcéɪʟʟ: I signify, pretend, explain.] A dart of love (is) piercing my body/ What is the point of telling it/ (For) there is no help in store for me/ Even if I won the love of my desiring.

[céɪm: step, degree, rank; ᴅúɪʟ: element, creature, anything created; ᴄʀoɪᵹ: foot, step; bonn: sole of foot; seᴀnᵹ: slender, svelte, graceful; sᴀoʀ: free, noble; mᴀʟᴀ: eyebrow; ᴅeᴀʟbᴀɪm: weave, form, construct.] These are the marks of the God of creation/ On the person to whom I give (my) love/ A slender foot and a noble, graceful sole/ A narrow eyebrow for which I construct verse.

[ᴅʟúċ: dense; ᴅúɪʟeᴀ̇ṁ: Creator; cʀom: bowed, drooping; cɪᴀb: tress; nɪᴀ̇ṁ: brightness, lustre, gloss, hue, tint; ᶠoʟċᴀɪm: I hide, cover, conceal.] The dense head of hair that is shelter from every weather/ (That) the Creator gave to her as glory/ Every drooping, curling ringlet of her tresses/ Having a lustre that overshadows the beauty of gold.

An béal tana is nuaide niam,
Nac zar dá zuaile a zlór,
'S a dá zruaid ar zné na zcaor,
Nár fuaiz act saor na sé slóz.

Stuad míonla na mailzead zcaol,
Ní sileab a hainm-se uaim,
Atá sin dom zoin dá zrád,
Do coil nac ál linn a luad.

Dá leacain leabra ar lí an aoil,
Do dealbad di mar ba cóir,
An bas bairr-zeal seada séim
Leaba réid na bfailzead n-óir.

An ríozan nac mbead do mnaoi
Mo searc ar n-a líonad lé
An Coimde ar n-a car i zclí,
Cá ní is doilze dam, a Dé.

12. **An bean do b'annsa liom fán nzréin**

An bean do b'annsa liom fán nzréin,
Is nár b'annsa léi mé ar bic,
'Na suide ar zualainn a fir féin,
Da cruaid an céim is mé istiz.

An zuirtín branair do rinneas dam féin,
Is me i bfad i bpéin 'na bun,
Zan az an bfear soin do táiniz indé,
Act a fuirse dó féin azus a cur.

Má rinnis branar zan síol,
Is fear mait den tír uait 'na bun,
Do freazras an Márta san am cóir,
Is do freastalas dóiz le n-a cur.

[nuᴀ: new, fresh; ıs nuᴀroe: freshest; nıᴀṁ: brightness, lustre; ʒné: characteristic, form, appearance; ꝼuᴀıʒım: I sew, stitch, bind; sᴀoʀ: mason, carpenter, craftsman.] The thin mouth of freshest gloss/ Whose voice is not close to her shoulders (*i.e. long-necked*)/ And her two cheeks of the appearance of berries/ That nobody wrought except the Craftsman of the Six Hosts.

[sᴄuᴀö: arch, princess; míonʟᴀ: gentle, mild, amiable; mᴀıʟʒeᴀö: ?; mᴀʟᴀ: eyebrow; áʟ: áıʟ.] Gentle princess of the narrow eyebrows (?)/ Her name shall not be dropped (*revealed*) from me/ That one (*she*) is wounding me for love of her/ By your leave, it is not pleasing to me to say (how).

[Leᴀᴄᴀ: slab, page, (cheek?, hand?); Leᴀbʀuıʒım: I smoothe, make even; Lí: colour; oeᴀʟbᴀım: I weave, form, construct; bᴀs: palm, hand, blade; bᴀʀʀ: tip (of fingers); seᴀoᴀ: slim, long; séıṁ: mild, fine, gentle; ꝼᴀıʟʒe: ring, jewel, buckle.] Two smooth hands of the colour of lime/ That were made for as was right/ The palm with bright, slender gentle fingers/ (That are) a ready bed for the golden rings.

[ʀíoʒᴀn: lady; seᴀʀc: love; Líonᴀım : I fill, give in full; coıṁoe: lord, protector; Coıṁoe: God; cᴀʀᴀım: I love; cʟí: stake, house-post, supporter, patron, hero; ᴅoıʟıʒ: sad, grievous, difficult; cá ní: ? cé ní, however ?] The lady who would not be a wife (to me)/ (Though) my love was given to her in full/ God love her and support her/ However difficult it is for me, O God.

12. The Woman Who Was Dearest To Me Under The Sun

[ᴀʀ ʒuᴀʟᴀınn: at the shoulder, beside.] The woman who was dearest to me under the sun/ And by whom I was not at all loved/ Sitting beside her own man/ It was a hard case, and I inside (the house, as well).

[bʀᴀnᴀʀ: fallow; ı mbun: looking after; péın: pain; ꝼuıʀse(ᴀċ): harrowing.] The little fallow field that I made for myself/ And I a long time in the labour of tending it/ That man who came yesterday had only/ But to till it for himself and sow it.

[ꝼʀeᴀsᴄᴀʟᴀım: I minister, prepare, await, attend; ᴅóıʒ: manner, state.] If you made fallow land without sowing it/ You are a good man of the country from you *(ridicule?)* looking after it! (*the fallow field*)/ – I answered the (month of) March (for sowing) at the right time/ And I attended (to it), ready for sowing it. *(First two lines of this verse are in the voice of a second party, commenting on previous two verses?)*

67

Is mairg do-ní branar go bráċ,
Ná beir fás fada dá ċuid féir,
Is an tan ċuadas-sa i bfad,
Gur coilleaḋ mo neaḋ tar m'éis.

Dá mbuḋ duine mise raġaḋ i bfad,
Is d'fáġfaḋ mo neaḋ tar m'éis,
Do ċuirfinn anál fá n-a bruaċ,
Do ċuirfeaḋ a fuaċ ar ʒaċ éan.

Cumann cealgaċ ag mnaoi,
Is cumann dearḃċa 'na ḋíol uaim,
Mise i nʒéibinn dá ʒráḋ,
Is ise ag caiṫeaṁ ʒaċ léim ar luas.

Cumann go dtéiʒeaḋ i sac,
Ní ḋéan feasta ar eagla an báis,
Is é beir mo ċroiḋe 'na ġual
An ʒráḋ fuar do bíos ag mnáib.

Níl bráṫair boċt gan hata cinn,
Báḋ ar tuinn ná tiġ ar tráiġ,
Mo ċorpán dá dtéiʒeaḋ 'san ʒcill,
Ag caoineaḋ im ċionn ní beaḋ na mná.

Fríd mo ċuṁa ní silid a rosc,
Greadaid siad a mbos go hard,
Le n-a méaraib fliuċaid a súil,
Is iomḋa lúib ins na mnáib.

Na creid cóṁráḋ mná,
'S ná ʒlac a láṁ i ʒceangal rúin,
Aire do cóṁairle an duine ġlic
Ní sin naċ mistide tú.

Is mairg atá mar atáim,
Is mairg do beir ʒráḋ leaṁ,
Is mairg do beas gan mnaoi,
'S dá ṁairg ag ná bíonn bean ṁaiṫ.

[mᴀɪʀʒ: woe, pity; coɪᴌᴌɪm: I geld, ruin, violate, cuckold; coɪᴌᴌeᴀö neᴀö éɪn: to violate the nest of a bird, to make a bird reject her nest.] It is a pity (for anyone) who makes fallow all the time/ Or who allows his grass to grow long (*go to seed, go to waste*)/ And the time I went away/ – That my nest was violated after me!

[ᴀnáᴌ: breath, influence.] If I were a person travelling far (away)/ And leaving my nest after me/ I would put a scent at its edge/ That would repel any (other) bird. *(Second voice, replying to previous verse?)*

[cumᴀnn, affection, acquaintance, sweetheart; ceᴀᴌʒᴀċ: stinging, deceitful; ᴅeᴀʀbċᴀ: certain; ᴅíoᴌ: satisfying, retribution; ʒéɪbeᴀnn: prison, trouble, great distress.] The woman's deceitful acquaintance/ It is a liaison definitely at my expense/ I (am) in trouble for love of her/ And she is throwing every jump at speed (*kicking her heels up*).

[sᴀc: sack.] A relationship (with any woman), until I go in a sack (*coffin*),/ I will not make ever again on fear of death/ It is what turned my heart into coal/ The cold love of women.

[cɪᴌᴌ: church, churchyard.] There is not a poor hatless friar (who is not in danger)/ Nor a boat at sea nor house on land/ My poor body, if it went to the graveyard/ The women would not be mourning on my behalf.

[ʒReᴀᴅᴀɪm: burn, strike, incite; ᴌúb: craft, deceit, trick.] Through my grief their eyes do not shed (tears)/ They wave their hands high/ With their fingers they wet their eyes/ There are many tricks in the women.

Do not believe the talk of women/ And do not accept their hand in a contract of love/ (Give) heed to the advice of the wise person/ That (is) a thing that you will not be worse for.

[ᴌeᴀṁ: impotent, tasteless, foolish.] It is a pity I am as I am/ It is a pity I give impotent love/ It is a pity for (a man) who is without a woman/ And it is two pities for (him who) has not a good woman.

Dá dtugtá póg do chailín deas,
Is go ndéarfadh leat "Is tú mo ghrádh",
Fá mar thiocfá scaoil uait,
Is ná bíodh ort gruaim tré mhnáibh.

Ná toigh bean ar a scéimh,
Go brionnair créad é a locht;
Tar éis iad do bheith dearg
Is searbh blas na gcaor gcon.

D'éaluigh Meadhbh ó Rígh Chruachna
De dhruim uabhair is macnais
Ris an rígh onórach do ghabh Éire
Is ná bíodh éad ort, a mharcaigh.

Nó an gcualas tú scéal Ghearóid Iarla
Mar éaluigh Cúntaois an chúil chiarta
Uaidh le meang is le cealg
Ré Lúróín ar feadh bliadhna.

D'éaluigh a bean ó Dháibhí an rí
Re hiomad coir agus cleas,
D'éaluigh a bean ó Fhionn féin,
Níl acht díth céille 'n-ár neart.

Guidhim Dia go lá an bhrátha
Dá gcuireadh cách dúinn i gcéill
Má tá i ndán dúinn go bráth stad
Leath olc na mban ná hinnstear é.

Dar Duinnín is dar Donn
Bun-ós-cionn liom gabhadh na mná,
Dá n-abrainn gur dubh é an fiach
Do thabharfaidís Dia nach eadh acht bán.

A fhir úd do ní coiméad ar do mhnaoi,
Cuir i gcríc dam créad an fáth.
Cionnus coiméadfas tú do bean
Dá dtéighir amach go bráth?

If you were to give a kiss to a pretty girl/ And she were to say to you *"You are my love"*/ As you would come (free), release (her) from you/ And let you not be sad because of women.

Do not choose a woman for her beauty/ Until you discover what is her failing/ After (=*despite*) they being red/ It is sour the taste of dog-berries.

[éaluiʒim: I escape, depart, elope; ʋe ʋ́ʀuim: over, because of; uaḃaʀ: pride, loneliness, eagerness for fight; macnas: (kindness, fondness), luxury, sensuality; maʀcaċ: horseman, knight, nobleman.] Maeve eloped from the king of Cruachain/ Because of pride and lust/ With the honourable king who took (all) Ireland/ So do not you be jealous, O knight! *(The second voice returning in this verse, and below?)*

[cúl: head of hair; ciaʀaim: I wax; meanʒ: deceit, guile; cealʒ: sting, treachery; lúʀoín: the little finger of the hand, an insignificant fellow?] Or did you hear the story of Earl Gerard/ How the Countess of the waxen hair eloped/ From him in deceit and treachery/ With the little fellow: for a year?

[coʀ: turn, throw, twist, move. *This verse refers to the romance of Gráinne (wife of Fionn Mac Cumhaill) and Diarmuid Ua Duibhne.*] His wife eloped from King David/ With many turns and tricks/ His wife eloped from Fionn himself/ There is but lack of wisdom in our strength.

I pray God, to the Day of Judgement,/: If everyone should tell us (their story)/ (And) if we are ever to stop: / Half the failing of women, let it not be told!

[ɼiaċ: raven; bun-ós-cionn: head over heels.] By Duinnín and by Donn!/ The women go topsy-turvy with me!/ If I were to say to them that the raven is black/ They would give (their oath to) God that it is not so, but white!

[coiṁéaʋ: keeping watch, guarding; cuiʀim i ʒcʀíċ: I accomplish, execute, realise.] You man, who keeps watch over your wife/ Convince me of the reason./ How do you keep watch over your wife/ If you ever go out?

Ḃeiṫ ḋá coiṁéaḋ is tú istiġ,
Ḋar liom ní maiṫ ḋo ċiall,
Ḋá n-iompuiġir léi ḋo ḋrom,
Riṫfeaḋ uait san cúil siar.

Ḋá mbeiṫṫeá is í taoḃ re taoḃ
Ḋo sméroḟeaḋ go claon a ḋearc,
Ḋá mbeiṫṫeá ós coṁair a ḋá súl
Ḋo ḃaġarḟaḋ mar siúḋ a ġlac.

Má ṫéiḋ sí go haifreann uait,
Ná fan an uair sin ḋá héis,
Ná bí roimpi ná 'na ḋiaiḋ,
"A Ċrann na Croiċe cá mbiaiḋ mé?"

Ná taoḃ t'anam re ḋo ṁnaoi,
Ġiḋ aiḋḃseaċ a caoi 's a ḋeor,
Fá ṫuirse ní bia aċt seal
Is ġeaḃaiḋ cúiċe an fear bias beo.

An clann so re bfuil ḋo ṡúil
Ḋá raiḃ tusa i n-úir na ġcnuṁ,
Ġaċ ar ṫacair tú re ḋo ré,
Cuirfiḋ go léir le sruṫ.

Le ḋrúis, le himirt, le hól,
Le suirġe na n-óg, le stáḋ,
Caiṫfiḋ an clann ḋo ċuiḋ
Is bia t'anam i mbruiḋ go bráṫ.

Ḋar an peann atá gan ġléas
Ḋá ḋtuiġṫeá-sa béas na mban,
Is an teaġasc ḋo ḃeirim uaim
Is ḋuine gan stuaim nár ġaḃ.

To be guarding her and you inside/ In my opinion your reasoning is not good/ If you turn your back on her/ She will run away from you out the back there.

[cLᴀon-ṡúıL: a fascinating or lovelorn glance or eye (*Dineen*).] If you and she were side by side/ She would craftily wink her eye/ If you were in front of her two eyes/ She would beckon thus with her hand.

[cʀoċ: gallows.] If she were to go to mass without you/ Do not wait that hour in her absence/ Do not be before her, do not be behind her/ "*O Tree of the Cross, where should I be?*"

[cᴀobuıɡ̇ım: I approach, trust; ᴀı̇ȯbseᴀċ: vast, dreadful; cuıʀse: affliction, fatigue, depression.] Do not entrust (the saving of) your soul (in Purgatory) to a woman/ No matter how great her weeping and crying/ You will be afflicted (dead) but for a while/ And she will get herself a man who is alive.

[súıL Le, súıL ᴀʀ: having an eye out for, expecation of; úıʀ: soil, the grave; cnuıṁ: maggot; cᴀcʀᴀım: I glean, gather, save; Le sʀuċ: "with the stream", for naught.] This family which you expect/ If you were in the clay with the maggots/ Everything you had accumulated in your time/ They would cast it to the winds!

[oʀúıs: adultery, lust; suıʀɡ̇e: courting; scᴀ́o: ? = scᴀ́ıo, stately woman; bʀoıo: captivity, bondage.] With debauchery, with gaming, with drinking/ With chasing after young women and mature women(?)/ The family would spend your portion/ And your soul would be forever in bondage (*in Purgatory, as nobody on earth would be gaining the sanctifying grace needed for release*).

[ɡ̇Léᴀs: device, means, style, fashion; béᴀs: custom, habit; scuᴀım: mental ability, prudence.] By this pen that is plain/ If you understood the habit of women/ And the teaching I give out/ It is an unwise person who would not accept (it).

A fir úd do rinne an duan,
Is cuir orm fuath gach mná,
Do dhallais m'intleacht ar fad
Do chosaint na mban ar cách.

Cosaint con ar tí cait,
Cosaint na bhfear ar na mnáibh,
Cosaint lachan ar linn
No faire na taoide ón dtráigh.

Beannacht ní thugaid na mná
Ar ainm an dáimh do rinne an duan,
Bean do geintear d'aon fhear amháin,
Agus bean eile do beir a slán fán sluagh.

Adhaint teineadh ar loch,
No carnáilt cloch i n-aghaidh cuain,
Cómhairle thabairt do mhnaoi buirb,
Nó buile ruibe ar iarann fuar.

Bean ghránna is gan í suairc,
A pósadh ba chruaidh an céim,
Créad an fáth go bpósfadh fear,
Ach an bean do b'áil leis fein.

Na tabair taob ris na mnáibh,
'S na tabair do dháil fá n-a neart,
Na creid uatha clog na mionn,
'S ná creid a dteanga liom leat.

Meabair an fáidh 's a dtáine 'dhraoithibh riamh
Mo cheann 'na phrás dá ndáile míle bliadhan,
Mo peann im láimh 's mé ag sár-chur síos mar iad,
Ar mheang na mná ní thráchtfaimís a dtrian.

Dá mba liom an peann do bí ceann ag Óibid seal,
Dá mba liom an ceann le n-ar mheabruigh Hómer stair,
Dá scaitinn-se an peann 's an ceann cé mor a leat,
Ní nochtfainn trian feall fallsacht ná fóirneart ban.

A Reply To Pierce By Another Poet:

[ᴅᴀʟʟᴀɪᴍ: I blind, confuse, puzzle; cosnᴀɪᴍ ᴀʀ: I defend from, I champion.] You, man there, who made the poem/ And put on me hatred for every woman/ You blinded my intellect altogether/ To the defence of women from everybody.

[ᴀʀ ᴄí: on the point of, on the track of, attacking.] Defence of a cat being attacked by a dog/ Is the defence of men against women/ Defence of a duck against water/ Or watching the tide from the shore.

[ᴈᴇɪɴɪᴍ: I beget, generate, make; ʙᴇɪʀɪᴍ sʟáɴ: I challenge.] The women do not give a blessing/ On the name of the poet who made the poem/ A woman (*one woman*) is made for one man only/ While another woman will take on a multitude.

[ᴀᴏ̇ɴᴀɪᴍ: I kindle, light; cᴀʀɴáɪʟ: heaping up, amassing; cuᴀɴ: bay, harbour, sea; cóṁᴀɪʀʟe: advice, admonition,direction; ʙoʀʙ: fierce, haughty, rough; ʀɪʙe: a hair, jot.] The kindling of a fire on a lake/ Or the heaping of stones against the sea/ Is the admonishing of a fierce woman/: Or the blow of a whisker against iron.

An ugly woman and she not jolly/ To marry her is a hard step!/ Why should a man marry/ (Any) but the woman he fancies?

[cuᴈᴀɪᴍ cᴀoʙ ʟe: I rely on; ᴅáɪʟ: a matter, affair, a hostile encounter; ᴍɪonn: oath; cʟoᴈ nᴀ ᴍɪonn: ?; ʟɪoᴍ ʟeᴀc: facing both ways, insincere.] Do not trust the women/ And do not take on their strength/ Do not believe (their) sound of oaths (?)/ And do not believe their false words.

[ɾáɾ̇o: poet, learned man, prophet; ᴅʀᴀoɪ: druid, magician, poet, learned man; pʀás: brass; ceᴀnn ᴅéᴀnᴄᴀ ᴅe ṗʀás: "head made of the best material"; ᴅáɪʟɪᴍ: I draw, dispense, administer, confer; ᴍeᴀnᴈ: deceit, guile.] The mind of the learned man and of all the druids who ever came (*were*)/ (Even if) I had a brain of brass, conferring about them (*women*) for a thousand years/ My pen in my hand and I putting down excellently how they (are)/ Of the guile of women we would not relate a third.

[ceᴀnn: tight, firm, powerful; ᴍeᴀʙʀuɪᴈɪᴍ: I recollect, perceive, ponder; cᴀɪᴄɪᴍ: I use; ɾeᴀʟʟ: treachery, falsehood, fraud; ɾᴀʟʟsᴀ: false, unreliable, deceptive; ɾóɪʀneᴀʀᴄ: great violence, oppression.] If I had the pen (writing ability) that was strongly Ovid's for a while/ (And) if I had the head with which Homer remembered history/ If I used the pen and the brain, though great (even the) half of it,/ I would not reveal a third of the deceit, falseness and oppressive ways of women.

75

Dá mbaḋ duḃ an ḟairrge, Dá mbaḋ cailce na cruaiḋ-cairrge
Dá mbaḋ meamram an spéar, Is dá mbaḋ pinn eiteḋe na n-éan,
Peann do ṫabairt i láiṁ gaċ fir, Do síol Áḋaiṁ is Éaḃaiḋ
D'ḟuigfdís uile dá n-éis, Trian olc mná gan faisnéis.

Ná déin-se tábaċt go bráṫ de ġníoṁarṫaib ban,
Aċt mar ṫráiġfeaḋ tráiġ nó tálfaḋ taoide ag teaċt,
Nó mar ċáit lá Márta i dtráṫ a timċealltar
Is go mbíonn a ngráḋ i ndá áit nó trí gan stad.

Níl file ná fáiḋ, bárd ná éigse triaċ,
Ná cuisle den dáiṁ dár táinig céim 'na ndiaiḋ,
Dá méid le ráḋ ar pár a saoṫar riaṁ
Do cuirfeaḋ síos cáil na mbáb dá léiġeanntaċt iad.

Duine éigin cct.

Annsaċt mná go bráṫ ná claoiḋeaḋ do ċiall,
Is fann a ngráḋ 's is fánaċ síleaċ iad,
Dream atá aṫáile ón ḃilinn iad,
'S is cam an fáṫ lér táṫaḋ croiḋe 'na gcliab.

Is sanntaċ ráiḋteaċ gáibṫeaċ maoiḋteaċ iad,
Mo ċeann 'na ṗrás dá ndáile míle bliaḋain,
Ar ṁeaḃair an fáiḋ 's a dtáine 'draoiṫib riaṁ
Ar ṁeabal na mná ní ṫráċtfaimís a dtrian.

An Freagra:

Aṁgar smáil ort 'fáiḋ big ċrín gan ċiall,
Do labair ar ṁnáib i n-áit nár ṫuill a dtrian;
Dá ḟeabas atáid, ó ṁnáib go mbí a dtriall,
'S le greann do Máire táinig Críost i gcliab.

[meᴀmrᴀm: parchment, scroll, manuscript; eιce: wing, feather; ꝼᴀιsnéιs: narrative, statement; éιs: track, trace; ꝺe éιs: lost, after.] If the sea were black, If the hard rocks were (soft as) chalks/ If the sky were parchment, And if the wings of birds were pens/ To put a pen in the hand of every man/ Of the seed of Adam and Eve/ All (of them) would leave out/ A third of the shortcomings of women, untold.

[cᴀḃᴀcc: value, validity, substance, importance; cRᴀιᵹιm: I ebb, subside; cᴀLᴀιm: I pour forth, flow (as milk from a breast); cᴀιc: chaff, sea-spray; cιmceᴀLLᴀιm: I compass, surround.] Do not ever make much of the actions of women/ But as the ebb-tide subsides or the rising tide flows/ Or as the dust of a (windy) March day as it blows about/ And that their affection is in two places or three, without rest.

[éιᵹse: poetry, literature, poet; cuιsLe: vein, pulse; ꝺᴀ́ṁ: tribe, following, party, academy; cuιsLe nᴀ ꝺᴀ́ιṁe: "the fount of the muses" (Dineen); pᴀ́R: parchment, document; cuιRιm síos: I describe; cᴀ́ιL: quality, reputation, character; báb: baby, maiden.] There is not a poet or prophet, bard or noble seer/ Or source of poetry that came after them in (their) footstep/: No matter how much ever to be said on the paper of their labours:/ No matter how learned they are, who could describe the character of the babes.

Somebody Composed:

[cLᴀoιꝺιm: I defeat, oppress, destroy; ꝼᴀnn: weak, unwilling; ꝼᴀ́nᴀc: aimless, useless; síleᴀc: subtle, unexpected, suspicious, doubtful; ᴀcᴀ́ιLe: ?; sᴀ́ιLe: sea-water, brine, the sea; ꝺíLe: flood, deluge; cᴀm: bent crooked, deceitful, erroneous; cᴀ́cᴀιm: I weld, join; cLιᴀḃ: basket, ribs, chest, bosom.] The love of a woman, let it never destroy your sense/ Their love is feeble, and they are useless and unreliable/ A crowd who are at sea (?) since the Deluge (is all) they (are)/ And false is the reason that a heart was joined to their chest.

[sᴀnncᴀc: covetous, greedy, miserly; Rᴀ́ιꝺceᴀc: sententious, gossiping; ᵹᴀιḃceᴀc: dangerous, exaggerating, costly; mᴀoιꝺceᴀc: boastful, begrudging; meᴀḃᴀL: shame, disgrace, (also, the female *pudenda*). *See verse on preceding page.*] They are greedy, talkative, aggravating, boastful/ If my head were brass and I were discussing them for a thousand years/ We would not relate a third of their disgracefulness.

The Reply:

[ᵹᴀR: profit, advantage, convenience, good turn; ᴀṁᵹᴀR: inconvenience, dissatisfied want; smᴀ́ιL: grief, vexation; smᴀ́L: ash, blemish, decay, insult, disgrace; cRíon: worn-out, old, withered, sapless; ᵹReᴀnn: fun, love, affection; cRιᴀLL: journey.] Trouble (and) vexation on you, you senseless, dried up little poet/ That spoke about women in a way in which not a third of them deserved/ No matter how wonderful they (the poets?) are, from women their journey (commences)/ And in esteem of Mary, Christ came to flesh!

77

13. Árduiġ do ṁeanma, a Ṁáġnuis

Árduiġ do ṁeanma, a Ṁáġnuis,
A túir ḋreacġlain ḋearcsáṁġlais,
A ṡlat ḟial iomlán i ġcat,
A iomráḋ cliar is cearrḃaċ.

A ḟir airmillte óġḃan,
A ċaistil ḟonn ḃraḋróoġlan,
A túir ċoscair, a ġríḃ ġrinn,
Is díḃ d'oscail ar n-inṫinn.

A ḋeaġláṁ ḋíolta ḟalaḋ,
A ḟáiḋ órta ar n-ealaḋan,
A ḟir ḟearḋa, a ġruaiḋ go nġoil,
Do ṁeanma iar n-uair árduiġ.

14. Díon, a Ċoimḋe, mo ċara

(Eoin Ua Callanáin do Ṗiaras Ḟeiritéar)

Díon, a Ċoimḋe, mo ċara
Mo ċoiġle re heascara,
Do luċt confaḋ ḟíoċḋa is fill
Sḃorfaḋ díoċra mar ḋriṫlinn.

A ḋíon fós feairrde sinne,
Ar anáirde inṫinne
A Ṗiarais 'sar ḟeirg ġaċ fir
'S ar ċeilg na ḃfiaḃras ḃfriṫir.

Maraiḋ múinte, mac feasaċ,
Staraiḋ cúirte cairdeasaċ,
Fearas fo ġean séanta ar ġcuiḋ
Naċ ro-néata aċt re namaiḋ.

Marcaċ cliste, ceann buiḋne,
Ann naċ miste ar muiniġne,
Ḃeiṫ go cráiḃṫeaċ caiṫṁeaċ caoin,
Maiṫṁeaċ náireaċ neaṁ-eascaoin.

13. Lift Your Spirits, Manus

[meᴀnmᴀ: mind, spirit, courage; cúʀ: tower; ᴅʀeᴀċ: countenance; ᴅeᴀʀc: eye; sᴀ́ṁ: peaceful; ʒlᴀs: fresh; slᴀc: staff, sceptre, youth, prince, chief; ıomlᴀ́n: whole, perfect; ıomʀᴀ́ᴅ: discourse, fame; ceᴀʀʀḃᴀċ: gambler, card-player.] Lift your spirits, Manus/ O tower of the pure countenance (and) the fresh, calm gaze/ O generous youth, perfect in battle/ O theme of cleric and gambler (*popular with all sorts*).

[mıllım: I destroy; ᴀ́rȯṁıllım: I destroy utterly; ᴀ ċᴀıscıl: ᴀ ċᴀısceᴀlᴀrȯe, O traveller; ꜰonn: tune, song; ꜰonn: fancy, pleasure, predisposition; ꜰonn: tract of land, earth; coscʀᴀım: I slaughter, triumph; ʒʀíoḃ: griffin, vulture, warrior, knight.] O man who devastates young women/ O traveller of lands with long clear roads/ O tower of triumph, O good-natured warrior/ It is to you I opened my mind.

[ꜰᴀlᴀ: grudge, spite, treachery; ᴅíolᴀım: I avenge; óʀᴀım: I gild, embellish; ıᴀʀ n-uᴀıʀ: after an hour, at last.] O good hand for avenging treachery/ O poet who adorns our art/ O manly man, O cheek with tears/ Your spirits, at last, raise.

14. Protect, O God, My Friend

(*Composed by* Eoin O Callanan for Pierce Ferriter. *Poem no. 6 above, by Ferriter, is dedicated to Eoin O Callanan, the physician*)

[coıṁᴅe: protector, God; coıʒle: coıʒéıle, companion, work-mate; conꜰᴀᴅ: fury, rapacity, greed; ꜰíoċ: feud, fight, wrath; ꜰeᴀll: treachery; sḃoʀᴀım: ? I spray, throw a shower of ?; ᴅíoċʀᴀcc: fervour, passion; ᴅʀıcle: spark, flash.] Shield, O God, my friend/ My companion against enemies/ (And) against people of greed, enmity and treachery/ He showers fervour like sparks (of fire).

[ᴀnᴀ́ıʀᴅe: on high, "uppity-ness", pride; ceᴀlʒ: sting, conspiracy, guile; ꜰʀıċıʀ: eager, peevish, fretful; ꜰıᴀḃʀᴀs ꜰʀıċıʀ: ? trembling fever?] O protector,: (for which) we (are) still better off:/ Against pride of intellect/ O Pierce, and (our protector) against the anger of every man/ And against the treachery of fretful fever (?)

[mᴀʀᴀrȯe: mariner; múınce: educated; mᴀc: son, fellow; scᴀʀᴀrȯe: historian; cúıʀce: ?= cúıʀceᴀṁᴀıl, courtly, gallant; cᴀıʀᴅeᴀsᴀċ: friendly; ꜰeᴀʀᴀım: I give out, bestow; ʒeᴀn: mouth, smile, affection; séᴀnᴀım: I deny, refuse, conceal; séᴀnᴀım: I bless, hallow; cuᴅ: portion, livelihood, wealth; neᴀċ: a person, someone; néᴀcᴀ: neat, nice, civil, amiable.] An expert mariner, a knowledgeable fellow/ A friendly, courtly historian/ He provides our living with hallowed affection (?)/ A very amiable person, except with enemies.

[cᴀıċṁeᴀċ: prodigal, generous; cᴀoın: gentle, kind; mᴀıċım: I forgive; mᴀıċṁeᴀċ: forgiving, indulgent; nᴀ́ıʀeᴀċ: modest.] A clever horseman, the leader of a troop (of soldiers)/ In him we are not the worse (for putting) our trust/ He is devout, generous, gentle/ Indulgent, modest, not unkind.

79

15. Cíꝺ iaꝺ an ċliar so 's an éigse as tír

(Ꝺo Piaras Feiritéar)

Cíꝺ iaꝺ an ċliar so 's an éigse as tír,
I mbliaꝺna re hiarratas séaꝺa is bíꝺ;
Ꝺo ċiapaꝺar siar mé 's ag téaċt arís
A ꝺtriallann ar Piaras Mac Éamuinn ꝺíoꝺ.

16. Ꝺ'ḟóbuir olc ꝺon urċar ċiar

(An Sagart Ꝺóṁnall Mac Taiꝺg an Ṡaráin cct ꝺo Piaras Feiritéar)

Ꝺ'ḟóbuir olc ꝺon urċar ċiar,
Ꝺo-ċuala i n-imlib aigian;
Lot láiṁe mo laoiċ ċailce,
Saoi fa sáiṁe subailce.

Ꝺon urċar ꝺo hinnleaꝺ lais,
Ꝺo fóbraꝺ príoṁ-lot Piarais,
Fearr ꝺúinn a ċéaċt mar atá,
Gan úiꝺ ar éaċt na ar iargná.

Molaꝺ mór ꝺo Ꝺia na nꝺúl,
Nár goineaꝺ an ġéag ġlanúr
A ḃeiċ beo gan ág gan oil,
Ꝺo beir an ceo ꝺo ċnocaib.

A láṁ ġasta ġléasta ġlinn,
Ꝺo ḟaġraꝺ ag scoil scríbinn,
Nár ċorċair ꝺo ḃloisc ar mball
Ꝺo ċoisc a urċair iomroill.

Láṁ ċruaiꝺ um loinn lasṁar,
Fear foirne na ḃfiangasraꝺ
Láṁ fial nár ḟill ó ḟile,
Ꝺar linn is mian maiġꝺine.

15. Who Are These Bards And Poets From The Country

(To Pierce Ferriter)

[cliar: band, company, chorus, bards, strolling singers, clergy; éigse: body of poets; as tír: from the (surrounding) country; séad: track, path, course.] Who are these bards and poets from (all over) the country/ This year, with requests for directions and food,/ They harassed me going west and coming back/ As they journey to Pierce, son of Eamonn!

16. Evil Nearly Came Of The Volley Back There

(The Priest Donal Mac Taidhg of Garrane composed, for Pierce Ferriter)

[*Ferriter was wounded in the siege of the castles held by the English under Thomas Spring, in Tralee in 1642. He constructed a siege weapon called the "sow" to attack the fortifications. The Sow was apparently a sort of Trojan Horse.*]

[fóbraim: I attack, approach, undertake, dare; d'fóbair: had like to, almost, nearly; urcar: shot, volley, cast, missile; tiar: to the west, over there (to the west); imeall: border, verge, edge, suggesting remoteness; aigean: ? = aigéan, ocean?; i gcéin: a long time ago, in the distance; cailce: chalk-white, beautiful; saoi: savant, expert, nobleman; sámh: composed, mild, tranquil, comfortable; subhailceach: virtuous, joyful.] Evil nearly came of that volley over there/ That I heard far away in the distance/ The wound to the hand of my fine warrior/ A nobleman who was tranquil and virtuous.

[innligim: I prepare, arrange, fix up, plan; téachtaim: I congeal, materialise, take shape, "become flesh"; teachtaim: I possess, hold, enjoy; úró: heed, attention; éacht: deed; iargnó: anguish, elegy, lament.] The volley that he prepared/ Nearly caused the main injury (death) to Pierce/ We prefer to keep him as he is/ Without expectation of (heroic) deed or anguish.

[goinim: I slay, wound; ág: valour, success, battle, luck; oil: reproach, blemish.] Great praise to God of Creation/ That the pure young prince was not slain/ (He) to be alive without success (?), without reproach/ Would take the fog from the hills.

[gasta: nimble, gléasta: prepared, equipped, neat; glinn: pure, plain, visible; fagraim: I fire, temper, heat, purge, purify; torcraim: I fall or perish, kill, am killed blosc: sudden loud noise; ball: limb, member, spot, place, implement; iomrall, confusion, error. [His nimble, neat, ready hand/ That was tempered in a literary school/ Your (bomb-)blast did not destroy our (*emphasis?*) limbs/ Because of its stray projectiles.

[um: with, about; loinn: joy, gladness, rapture; lasmhar: radiant; fear foirne: leader; fiangasrad: band of Fianna; fillim ó: I return, make a return for, pay back.] A firm hand, with radiant pleasure/ The leader of the band of heroes/ A generous hand that (never) refused a poet/ To our mind, the (heart's) desire of (any) maiden.

81

Tá an bean ag breiṫ buiḋe,
An feallsaṁ 's an fiannuiḋe,
Maiṫ a beiṫ gan ġoiṁ gan ġoin
'Na leiṫ gan ḋoiġ gan ḋiaċoir.

A ḃeiṫ gan ceirḋ gan cinneas
Beiḋ um oileán airṁilleas
Éiḋe cosnaiṁ ceall is cliar
Maiṫ leam ḋon bos-ġlan ḃairr-ḟiar.

Do Ċiarraiġe na mbroġ mbán,
ḃoir fear is mnaoi is macáṁ,
Na ġuil-si ón gcaṫslóġ do ċuir
Cuirsi is aṫḃrón d'ḟóbuir.

17. Ní truaġ galar aċt gráḋ folaiġ

(Cum Meiġ Ruiséil)

Ní truaġ galar aċt gráḋ folaiġ,
Uċ is fada gur smuain mé,
Ní biaḋ níos sia gan a noċtaḋ
Mo ġráḋ folaiġ don tseang séiṁ.

Tugas gráḋ ná féadaim d'ḟolaċ,
Dá folt coclaċ, dá rún leasc,
Dá malainn ċaoil, dá rosc gorm,
Dá ḋéiḋ socair, dá ġnúis ġeal.

Tugas fós, gion go n-aḋṁuim,
Gráḋ mar m'anam dá píp réiḋ,
Dá ġuṫ ró-ḃinn, dá béal blasta,
Dá huċt sneaċtṁar, dá cíċ ġéir.

Uċ, monuar ní ċéiḋ i nḋearmaḋ,
Mo ġráḋ scamalaċ dá corp geal,
Dá troiġ slím-ċeart tráċt-ċana,
Dá ġáire riġin, dá croḃ tais.

[buröe: thanks; peaLLsaṁ: philosopher; piannuröe: soldier; ʒoiṁ: venom, sting; ı Leıċ: by way of, as if it were, in view of; ꝺoıʒ: pang, dart of pain; ꝺıaċaıR: sorrow, trouble.] The woman is giving thanks/ (As are) the philosopher and the soldier (*all sorts of people*)/ (That it is) good that you are (now) without venom, without wound/ As (you are now) without pain or trouble.

[ceröm: attack of illness, pestilence; um oıLeán: throughout (the) island; aröṁıLLeas: aröṁıLıs, very sweet, lovely; éroe: clothing, armour; Leam: Lıom; pıaR: awry, twisted; baıRR: tips (of fingers).] (For him) to be without pain or illness/ There will be, throughout (this) sweetest (of) island(s),/ The defensive armour of church and cleric/ Dear to me your pure hand with twisted fingers!

[bRoʒ: house, mansion, castle, town; bán: white, fair, beloved, beautiful, empty; ʒoL: weeping, cry; caccsLóʒ: army.] To Kerry of the fair mansions/ Between man and woman and youth/ The cries that the army gave (*when you were wounded*)/ Did forbode affliction and great sorrow.

17. Illness Is No Misfortune Compared With Hidden Love

(For Meg Russell)

[ıs cRua: it is a pity, it is unfortunate; poLaċ: hiding, concealing; smuaınım: smaoınım, I think; seanʒ: slender, graceful; séiṁ: mild, tender, pleasing.] Illness is no misfortune compared with undisclosed love/ Och, it is long I have thought that/ (But) I will no longer be without revealing/ My hidden love to the graceful, tender lady.

[poLc: tresses; coċLaċ: ?; coċaLL: hood, cowl; cocánaċ: in curls; Leasc: lazy, slow, measured, stately; Rún: mystery, disposition, love, sweetheart; maLa: eyebrow; socaıR: even, plain, smooth, calm.] I gave love that I cannot hide (any longer)/ To her hooded (*covered*?) hair, to her reserved disposition/ To her thin eyebrows, to her blue eyes/ To her even teeth, to her bright countenance.

[ʒıon ʒan; ʒıon ʒo: without that, even though not; píp: throat?; ʒéaR: sharp, keen, well-defined.] I gave also, even were I not to admit it/ Love like my soul to her smooth throat/ To her so sweet voice, to her delicious mouth/ To her snowy-white bosom, to her pointed breasts.

[ní: a thing; scamaLLaċ: dark, cloudy, melancholy; sLím: slender, smooth, spruce; cRáċc: faring, going, tread, the sole of the foot; Rıʒın: tough, slow; ʒáıRe Rıʒın: unwilling smile; cRob: claw, hand; caıs: damp, soft, tender, compassionate.] Och, alas, a thing that is forgotten (by her)/ My melancholy love for her bright body/ For her truly slender, narrow-soled feet/ For her diffident smile, for her tender hand.

bíoö nár fionnaö riaṁ roiṁe
Méro mo ċumainn oí tar cáċ,
ní bfuil, ní biaıö is níor imtıȝ
bean is truıme ȝoro mo ȝráö.

Faoa ár ȝcoṁtrom ó céile

Faoa ár ȝcoṁtrom ó céile,
Mise is mo céile ċumainn,
Mise ȝo noíoȝrais uimpe,
Is ȝan í ȝo soilbir umainn.

Ȝo otréiȝfeaö mise ar sároöreas
níl ann aċt ainbfıos céille;
'S ná tréiȝfinn-se mo bean ċumainn,
'S a teaċt ċuȝam 'na léine.

Aice is ualaċ éaotrom,
A searc, is tréan trom orum,
'S ná oeineann sé ȝoıṁ oon ȝalar,
Ó céile is faoa ár ȝcoṁtrom.

18. **A Dıa na mbuaö an truaȝ leat mise mar táim**

A Öia na mbuaö an truaȝ leat mise mar táim,
I bpríosún fuar is naċ mór ȝo bfeicim an lá,
An braon bíonn ċuas i n-uaċtar lice ȝo háro
Aȝ tuıtim im ċluas is fuaim na tuınn lem sáil.

19. **Beir uaim-se friotal ċum riöire Duıöneaċ sıar**

beir uaim-se friotal ċum rıoire Öuıbneaċ sıar,
'S innis oó ar feaö m'uireasba ȝo bfuilim féin buıöeaċ oo Öıa;
ní fearroe mise ar ıbeas oo na fíontaıb rıaṁ
Seaċ uisce na ruıoe seo is mise innte sínte sıar.

[fionnaim: I know, understand, discover; cumann: affection, love, society; imcigim ar: I happen to, befall; trom: heavy, pregnant, sad, serious.] Let it be (Suppose it is so) that it was never before known/ The greatness of my love for her above all (others)/ There is not, there will not be, and there did not happen/ A woman who stole my love (*i.e. without require*) so seriously.

Our Unequal Love

[comtrom: an equal weight, equality, justice, fair play; céile: fellow, companion, mate; díográis: affection, loyalty, enthusiasm, passion; soilbir: cheerful, happy, optimistic, sociable.] Our measures (of love) are far (different) from each other/ I and my fellow sweetheart/ I with passion about her/ And without her being happy around me.

[tréigim: I forsake, desert, give up; tréigim ar: I give (something) up for.] That I should forsake (her) for wealth/ There is nothing in that except nonsense/ And I would not give up my sweetheart/ Were she to come to me in her shirt (*in poverty*).

[goim: venom, malice, hurt.] She has a light load/ (My) love for her, it is a heavy load on me/ And does it not make the fever (of love) poisonous/ Unequal to each other are our measures (of love).

18. O God Of Excellence, Do You Pity Me As I Am

[buadó: victory, success, virtue, excellence, attribute; tonn: wave; sáil: sawing, cutting.] O God of Excellence, am I a(n object of) pity to you as I am/ In a cold prison, and I shall hardly see the (next) day/ The drop above that is on top of a slate on high/ Falling in my ear and the sound of the ocean-waves cutting (through) me.

19. Take From Me A Word West To The Knight Of Duibhne

[friotal: (spoken) word; uireasba: deficiency, need, poverty, want; ní fearroe liom: I do not prefer, care; ibim: I drink, quaff; seac: compared with; roroe: bog-water.] Take from me, to the west, a word to the Knight of Corca Dhuibhne/ And tell him, while I am in want, that I am thankful to God/ I do not prefer all the wines I ever quaffed/ Compared with the bog-water, and I stretched out in it here!

20. Ní hé marbaḋ an Dúin ḋo ḃrúiġ mo ṁuineál riaṁ

Ní hé marbaḋ an Dúin ḋo ḃrúiġ mo ṁuineál riaṁ
Ná a nḋearnaḋ liúm i gciuṁais an Oileáin Tiar,
Acht an óiġ-ḃean ṁúinte búrḋ na gcocán gciar
Ná ḋeaġas 'á ḟiosruġaḋ ar ḋtúis ná im ḋonán liaċ.

21. A riḋire na circe 's a' ġanḋail ġé

A riḋire na circe 's a' ġanḋail ġé
Mise 'gus tusa ar gaċ taoḃ ḋen ṁéis;
Ní mar sin ḋo ḃinn-se is mo ṁuinntear féin,
Acht 'nár gcúigear ar fiċo is ba ġann liom é.

22. Do ċonnac aisling ar maiḋin an lae ġil

(Marḃna Piarais Feiritéir)

Do ċonnac aisling ar maiḋin an lae ġil,
Do ḃris mo ṡuan ḋo ḃuaiḋir mo ċéaḋfaḋ,
Tug mo ċroiḋe go claoiḋte tréiṫ-lag,
Is cé go mairim, ḋo ṁairḃ go léir mé.

Fóḋla i gceas i ḃfaḋ roiṁ Éirinn,
Ag caoi 's ag caoineaḋ 's ag géar-ġol,
A gnaoi ar mí-lí gur ċréig sí,
'S a cruṫ geal ar ḋaṫ nár ġléigeal.

Í líonta 'cuṁa go dubaċ ḋéaraċ,
I nḋeoiḋ a fear is flaiṫ na féile,
Ag sníoṁ a glac 's ag staṫaḋ a céiḃe,
Gan bríġ go lag le neart a héigin.

Fiafruiġim ḋí ḋo'n ḟuiġle is séiṁe
Cá cúis ċaointe ag mnaoi Cuinn Céaḋċaṫ,
Nó cia an tír 'nar fríṫ na scéalta
Tug fá scís na tíorṫa i n-éinḟeaċt.

20. It Was Not The Slaughter Of The Fort That Ever Squeezed My Neck

[cıuṁaıs: edge, border; búṙö: gentle, affable, gracious; cocán: curl (of hair); cıaʀ: waxen; ná ɒeaɤas: that I did not go; ɒonán: an enfeebled person.] It was not the Slaughter of the Fort that ever squeezed my neck/ Nor what was done to me on the edge of the West Island/ But the mannerly, gracious young woman of the glossy curls/ That I did not go enquiring after at first, or (even) as a grey enfeebled old man.

21. O Knight Of The Hen And The Gander

O knight of the hen and the gander goose/ Me and you at each side of the dish!/ That was not the way I was, nor my people ever/ But twenty five of us, and that was little enough for me!

22. I Saw A Vision On The Morning Of The Bright Day

(Elegy for Pierce Ferriter)

[buaṙöʀım: I bother, vex, torment; céaɒʀaö: sense, faculty, understanding.] I saw a vision on the morning of the bright day/ That broke my peace and vexed my mind/ It made my heart defeated and feeble/ And though I am alive, it killed me utterly.

[ʀóɒla: Ireland, *a female spirit representing Ireland*?; ceas: affliction, dread; caoi: weeping; ɤnaoı: beauty, comeliness; mí-lí: bad colour.] (The vision was) Fódla afflicted for a long time before (all) Ireland/ Weeping and lamenting and crying sorely/ Her beauty deserted for a sickly hue/ And her bright form a colour that was not shining.

She, filled with sadness, gloomy, tearful/ After her husband who is a lord of hospitality/ Wringing her hands and pulling her hair/ Without strength, and weak from the force of her predicament.

[ʀuıɤle: speech, words; Conn Céaɒċaċaċ: Conn of the Hundred Battles, *a king of Ireland*; ʀʀıoċuıɤım: I attend, serve; scíos: weariness, fatigue, grief.] I ask her in the mildest of words/ What is the cause of lamentation of the wife of Conn of the Hundred Battles/ Or what is the country that did not attend to the reports/ That brought to sorrow (all) the countries together.

Do ráiḋ an bean ḋár b'ainm Éire,
Cá tír i mbíṫí ar ḋíṫ céille,
Mar ná fuarais cluas le héisteaċt
Ar éag an ḟir lér ṫuit na céaḋta.

Sirim ort, má's toil leat féaċaint
Ar mo ċás ó ṫárla i nḋaor-ḃruiḋ,
Réiḋ mo ċeist is beir mé a baoġal,
Is ḋeiṁniġ ḋam cár ċeasta an té sin.

A ḋubairt Fóḋla do ġlór nár ḃréaġaċ
Taoḃ le loċ do croċaḋ an t-éarlaṁ,
Do sloinntear ón gcríċ do ċinn ar Éirinn,
Ar an ḋtulaiġ ḋá ngoirtear Cnoc Caoraċ.

Bíoḋġaim ar scaoileaḋ an scéil sin,
Is ṫugas aṁarc ar ḟairsinge an tsléiḃe,
Do ráiḋ gaċ fir ḋá ḋtig 'na ḋtréin-riċ,
Is fíor ar ċan an bean ba héigneaċ.

Buailim m'uċt, do ġoin go haeḋiḃ mé
Bás an tí do ċinn go héaċtaċ,
'S a beiċ anoċt fá ḃruiḋ 'na aonar
Ag bárḋa an Ruis 'ġá ċur i n-éaġaiḃ.

A ṫír Ḋuibneaċ, is ḋaoib is céasta,
Sib 'na ḋeoiḋ naċ ḋóiġ gur saoġalaċ,
Fál bar ḋtórraṁ, stór bar laoċ mear,
Croḋ bar n-óg-ḃan, lón bar léiġeann-ṁac.

An té ba hursa is do b'urraḋ is do b'ḟéiteaṁ,
Ag ḋíon bar gcreaċ is teaċ bar ḋtréaḋa,
Is do bar nḋíon ar ṁíle léir-scrios
Ag ḋíol bar bfiaċ 's 'na nḋiaiḋ gan éileaṁ.

Atáiḋ a ḋúnta i gcuṁa gan faeseaṁ
Is baile an Ḋaingin cé'r ḋeacair a ṫraoċaḋ,
'S a ċóṁarsain ag cóṁ-ġol go héigneaċ,
Is na trí tíorṫa tré n-a ċéile.

[ᴅᴀ́ʀ ʙ’ᴀɪɴм ... ᴄᴀ́ ᴄíʀ: whose name ... which country; ? *recte* ɢᴜʀʙ ᴀɪɴм ... ᴅon ᴄíʀ: that the name ... of the country (?).] The woman said that the name was Ireland/ Of the country in which there was lack of reason/ As you had not an ear (*the means*) to hear/ Of the death of the man by whom hundreds fell (in battle).

[sıʀɪм: I seek, investigate, entreat; ᴄeᴀsᴄuıɡɪм: I am wanting *or* missed, I die.] I entreat you, if you will, to look/ At my case as I find (myself) in a bad way/ Solve my problem and save me from danger/ And confirm to me where did that person die.

[éᴀʀʟᴀṁ: patron, head of a community, noble person; cınnɪм ᴀʀ: I go beyond, surpass; cınneᴀnn oʀм: I fail.] Fódla said in a voice that was not false/ Beside a lake the nobleman was hanged/ (The lake) is called after the country that bested Ireland/ (He was hanged) on the mound that is called Sheep's Hill. (*The king of* ʟoċ ʟéın *was not subject to the King of Cashel, ruler of Munster.*)

[ʙíoóɢᴀıм: I startle, become excited; ᴀʀ ḟᴀıʀsınɢe: on the extent of, all around; éıɢneᴀċ: violent, distressful.] I start up at the issuing of this news/ And I look all around the hill/ Every man who came running swiftly said/ It is true what the woman related, who was distressful.

[ᴀe: the liver; ᴄí: ᴄé; cınnɪм: I excel; éᴀċᴄᴀċ: deed-doing, powerful, magnificent.] I strike my breast, (the news) wounded me to the heart/ The death of the person who excelled magificently/ For him to be, this night, imprisoned alone/ By the warden of Ross, putting him to death. (*The vision appeared on the morning of the execution.*)

[Coʀcᴀ ᵭuıbne: *part of the Dingle peninsula*; céᴀsᴄᴀ: tormented, vexed, crucified; sᴀoɢʟᴀċ: living, long-lived; ḟᴀ́ʟ: hedge, protection; ᴄóʀʀᴀṁ: wake, attendance, funeral, party, guard; sᴄóʀ: store, treasure; cʀoᴆ: cattle, chattels, compensation, dowry; ʟón: provisions, food.] O land of Corca Dhuibhne, you are tormented/ You, after him (his death), it is unlikely you will live/ The guardian of your wakes, the treasure of your great warriors/ The dowry of your young women, the provision of your scholars.

[uʀsᴀ: prop, doorpost; uʀʀᴀᴆ: chattel, utensil; ḟéıᴄ: vein, nerve, sinew, muscle; ḟıᴀċ: debt; éıʟıɢɪм: I look for, sue for, demand, call to account.] The person who was the prop, the wealth and the strength/ Your protection from destruction and the shelter of your herds/ and who (was) your defence against a thousand total ruinations/ Settling your debts and not calling (you) to account afterwards.

[ᴄʀᴀoċᴀıм: I abate, exhaust, subdue, hunt down.] His castles are in grief without relief/ And (also) the town of Dingle that is hard to subdue/ And his neighbours weeping together distressfully/ And the three countries (*baronies?*) in confusion.

89

Dún Caoin ba haoibinn ré néallaib,
Is Dún an Óir nár cóir do créigean,
Dún Úrla i gcúl gur léir-cuir,
Is Dún Meṁóreaċ taróbseaċ, taob-ġeal.

Lá dá ḃreaca ag an ḃfaraire féata
I gcuan nó i gcaladö-ṗort daingean na hÉireann
Caḃlaċ mara do b'armaċ éroeaċ
Dá ḃroḃaö, dá ḃreannaö, dá reacaö, 's dá réaḃaö,

Cé do ṁeasfaö ná mairfeaö aċt tréiṁse
An tí ba ċosṁail le Hector na Trae ċoir
Nó le Hearcuil ag leaöraö laoċ mear
Ag teaċt don baile 's a banna gan daor-loc?

Go ló an luain ní luaiöfear laoċ mear
Dul i ngleo nó i gcóṁrac aonair
Ris an gcuraö nár b'furas a ċraoċaö,
Mar Coin Culainn do ciorrbaö ar féiclb.

Dreiteaṁ ceart é i measc a ġaolta,
Ar scríbinn ġasta ba cneasta an cléireaċ,
Caoin re seanaib, tais re béitib,
Lag le fann is teann re tréanaib.

Captaoin cróöa beoöa i n-éaċtaib,
Mars ar eolas, leoġan ar laoċas,
Ar clár bócna leor a tréine,
Seabac na n-oileán ar ġabáil éanlaiċ.

Impire ar uaisle, Guaire ar féile,
Marcaċ líoṁta, i ngníoṁarċaib stéaöṁar!
Saiġoiúir fír-iúil ar éaċtaib,
Máiġistir pionnsa is Fionn na Féinne.

Ciste rúin tú is úird na cléire,
Gráö na maiġdean mbraiġro-ġeal mbéasaċ,
Orċóir an dána ós Clár Éibir,
Oröe múinte is clú na héigse.

[néaʟʟ: cloud, exhalation, mood, "vapours", rage, frenzy, exasperation; cuιrιm: I put, plant, bury; cuιrιm ι ʒcúʟ: I renounce, forsake; caιöbseaċ: visible, magnificent, attractive.] Dún Caoin that was beautiful (now) under clouds/ And (also) Dún an Óir that should not have been abandoned/ Dún Úrla being forsaken/ And (also) Dún Meidhreach, magifnicent, bright-walled. (*Referring to his castles and estates; see previous verse.*)

[ɸaraιre: brave fellow, soldier, watchman; ɸéaca: comely; caöʟaċ: body, frame, navy; ɸoöaιm: I attack; ɸeannaιm: I flay, plunder; reιcιm: I sell at a loss, squander; reacaιm: ? I wreck?/ réabaιm: I rend, burst.] One day there was seen by the comely watchman/ ín a harbour or in a well-defended port of Ireland/ A naval fleet that was armed and armoured/ (And he was) attacking it, plundering it, wrecking it and destroying it. (*According to Dinneen (1934 edition), the English State Papers for the year 1650 record a case brought by Roger Peterson on behalf of Peter Peterson, captain of the ship The Fortune, against the Marquis of Ormonde, for the looting of his ship by Captain Pierce Ferriter and his followers when the ship took shelter in Dingle Bay. On the 28th of February 1650, Lord Inchiquin wrote that Major Dominic Ferriter (Pierce's son) boarded the ship with his followers and, remaining on board for a few days, preserved it from destruction by the storm; and that Major Ferriter would make certain recompense to Peterson.*)

[ʟeaoraιm: I mangle, beat; banna: company, band.] Who would that (he) would live only a (short) while/ The person who was similar to Hector of Troy (to the) east/ Or to Hercules, smiting great warriors/ And (always) coming home without his band (of soldiers) being completely destroyed.

[ʟá an ʟuaιn: the Day of Judgement; ʟuaιöιm ʟe: I refer to, compare with; curaö: warrior, knight, hero; craocaιm: I subdue, exhaust; cιorrbaιm: I hew, cut, take away, destroy; ɸéιċ: vein, sinew.] To the Day of Judgement no great warrior will be compared/: in going into (general) battle or in single combat./ With the hero who was not easily subdued/ (Being) like Cú Chulainn who hacked at (the) sinews (of his enemies).

[cneasca: modest, mild, humane; cʟéιreaċ: cleric, clerk, man of letters; caoιn: kind; caιs: mild; bé: maid, woman, Muse; ʟaʒ: gentle; ɸann: weak; ceann: firm.] An honest judge he was, among his relatives/ At clever writing, he was a decorous literary man/ Kind to the old, tender with women/ Gentle with weak, firm with the strong.

[beoöa: lively, active; cʟár bócna: the plane of the ocean; leor: sufficient, plentiful; ʒaöáιʟ: capture.] A brave captain, active in exploits/ A Mars in knowledge, a lion in heroism/ On the plane of the ocean his fortitude was plentiful/ (He was) the hawk of the (Blasket?) islands in the capturing of birds. (*The Ferriters held the Blasket Islands as hereditary hawk-breeders for their Geraldine overlords.*)

[ʒuaιre: a king of Connacht, noted for his generosity; ʟíońċa: polished, scéaöńar: equine; íúʟ: eoʟ, knowledge; éaċc: exploit; éaċca: tactics?; pιonnsa: fencing.] An emperor in nobility, a Guaire in hospitality/ A polished horseman in equine exploits/ A soldier truly knowledgeable in tactics/ A master of fencing, a Fionn of the Fiann.

[cιsce: chest, store; rún: secret, mystery; úιro: óιro?; cʟιar: band, company, clergy, religious orders, bards, chorus; óιrιm: I gild, embellish; ós: mouth; Cʟár Éιbιr: *figurative term for Ireland*; cʟú: fame, honour, glory, ornament.] Store of secret knowledge and order(?) of the bards/ The love of bright-bosomed, mannerly maidens/ The embellisher of the poem, the voice of the plain of Éibhear/ Enlightened teacher and adornment of poetry.

Ꝼile 'gus uġdar múinte ı mḃéarla,
Léiġteoir blasta ar ḟearsa Gaeḋilge,
Tuigseaċ Larone ıs staire Gréigıs,
Ꝼear cómaḋ-ċur go cóiṁ-ḋeas san Réiḋteaċ.

Do ḃí sé ḟáilteaċ cráiḃṫeaċ ḋéarcaċ,
Do ḃí tabarṫaċ bronntaċ béasaċ,
An cian do ṁair deag-ṁac Éamuinn,
Ḃó na mboċt ıs croḋ na cléire.

Ar ċeannaċ ḟíona síoda 's éadaiġ,
Ar ḋáil maoine diġe 'gus méaṫ-ṁairt,
Ar ċaiṫeaṁ ḟleiḋe 's ḟéasta 'na aol-ḃrog
Níor ċug sé bárr ná tár d'éinneaċ.

Dá mbeinn ċorḋċe ag ríoṁ do ṫréiṫe,
Ag áireaṁ ar ḋéárlais do ṡéadaiḃ,
Do leaṫ Moġa 'gus Conn na gcéad-ċaṫ
A gcur síos ı gcríċ níor léir liom.

Is boḋar 's ıs balb an Ḃanba ıt éagmuis,
Do ċaill a clú, do ṁúc a daonnaċt,
Na Danair gaċ lá ag gabáil a saor-ḟlaiṫ,
Is ıad ḟá ḃruid ı ríoċt naċ saoġuin.

Do luiġe, do ṡíneaḋ, do ċéad-ċur
Tug an ċliar ḟá ċıaċ ı mbaoġal,
Tar muir do ċuir an biṫ braonaċ
D'ḟearaiḃ áilne 'on Spáin dá dtraocaḋ.

Moċean feart 'nar ċaisce t'aol-ċorp,
Do ḋá ċaoḃ cailce ar ḋat na géise,
Do ḋá ċroiġ tana cearta séiṁe,
Is do ḋá ċaol-ṁala ós leacain ġléigil.

A Ṗiarais m'anama ó ċailleas rem ré tú,
Is ná ḟuil aiseag ar ṁarb dá n-éagann,
Triaṫ na n-aingeal dot ġairm a daor-ḃruid,
Suas go Ḟlaiṫeas go Caṫair an Éin-Ṁic.

[bLᴀꞅᴛᴀ: tasty, fluent, elegant; ꝑeᴀꞃꞅᴀ: verse; Ᵹꞃéıᵹıꞅ: the Greek language; cómᴀᴅ: *the last two lines of a quatrain in ᴅáɴ ᴅíꞃeᴀċ, hence,* poetry *in general*; ꞃéıᴅᴛıᵹım: I adjust, arrange, smoothe, solve, scan(?).] A poet and distinguished author in English/ Elegant in the reading of Irish verse/ Interpreter of Latin, and of history in Greek/ A man who wrote verse which scanned tastefully.

[cꞃoḃ: cattle, chattels, dowry; cLıᴀꞃ: clerics, clergy, bards; bó: cow, "provider".] He was welcoming, devout, almsgiving/ He was generous, giving, urbane/ The while Eamonn's good son lived/ (He was the) provider of the poor and the wealth of the bards.

[ᴅáıL: distributing; méᴀċ: fat; mᴀꞃᴛ: beef; bᴀꞃꞃ: top, supremacy; bꞃoᵹ: castle, mansion.] At buying wine, silk and clothing/ At distributing wealth, drink and fat beef/ At throwing parties and feasts in his white mansion/ He gave supremacy to nobody.

[ᴅeᴀꞃLᴀcᴀım: I give, bestow; ꞅéᴀᴅ: article of value; Leᴀċ ṁoᵹᴀ, Leᴀċ Ċᴜınn: *two ancient divisions of Ireland, northern and southern, respectively*.] If I were ever counting your (good) qualities/ (Or) reckoning the bestowal of your valuables/ To Mogh's Half and Conn of the Hundred Battles' (Half)/ Their full description I could not see.

[ꞅᴀoᵹᴜın: ꞅéᴀᵹᴀınn, distinguished, accomplished, noble.] Ireland is deaf and dumb without you/ Her glory lost, her humanity extinguished/ The Danes (*savages*) each day capturing her noble lords/ And they imprisoned in ignoble condition.

[Lᴜıᵹe: lying, being ill, decline; ꞅínım: I stretch, lay out, knock down, prostrate; cıᴀċ: oppression, hoarseness, asthma; bıᴛ: world, life, existence; bꞃᴀonᴀċ: tearful, sorrowful.] Your decline, your prostration, your fall/ Brought the bards under oppression (and) in danger/ The sorrowful existence sent overseas/ Splendid men, despatched to Spain.

[ꝑeᴀꞃᴛ: grave, tomb; ᴛᴀıꞅcım: I store, treasure; ᵹéıꞅ: swan; ceᴀꞃᴛ: right, proper; óꞅ Leᴀcᴀın: óꞅ cıonn Leᴀcᴀın, over the cheeks, face.] My regards to the grave in which your white body was stored/ Your two white sides the colour of the swan/ Your two thin, proper, pleasing feet/ And your two thin eyebrows over the bright countenance.

[ᴀıꞅeᴀᵹ: recovery] O Pierce of my soul, since you died in my (life-)time/ And as there is no recovery for the dead when they pass away/ May the leader of the angels call you from captivity/ Up to Heaven, to the City of the Only Son.

The So-Called Rebellion Of 1641 And Its Cromwellian Outcome

Pierce Ferriter was a Norman Irish gentleman in West Kerry in the middle of the 17th century. And the mode of being of a Norman Irish gentleman led him in action to be both an exuberantly Gaelic poet and a soldier in what is called the Irish Rebellion of 1641. His Norman aspect had no bearing on his being a soldier. The MacCarthys, O'Sullivans etc. were all soldiers alongside him in that 'Rebellion'. But MacCarthy and O'Sullivan gentlemen did not write poetry. They had poets who did that for them. The great O'Sullivan poet did not emerge until the late 18th century, generations after the traditional social structures of Gaelic life had been broken by Cromwellian and Williamite totalitarianism, and the remnants had merged themselves into something new within the swampland of Slieve Luacra. Eoghan Ruadh was an itinerant day-labourer and vagabond, and his clan inheritance had been comprehensively lost for three generations, when he gave the O'Sullivan name a prime position among the poets. But Ferriter was a poet while still in possession of his ancestral acres.

The extensive Gaelic/Norman *rapprochement* that happened in parts of Munster was not simply a merger. It was said that those Normans "became more Irish than the Irish themselves". And I suppose it could be said that a Norman Irish gentleman who became his own poet had, in a sense, become more Irish than the Irish themselves. A McCarthy was entirely satisfied with having a poet, but Ferriter had to experience the existence of Irish life more comprehensively by himself *being* a Gaelic poet. The Normans tended to be adaptable, imitative and thorough.

And there was of course a strong literary development amongst Ferriter's cousins in England in the first half of the 17th century—the Monarchist gentry who came to grief in the Civil War and were lost without trace in the destructive vulgarity unleashed by the Glorious Revolution of 1688—from the urbane Satires of John Donne, through the "metaphysical poetry" in which the flesh was not lost, to the constitutional theory of Sir Robert Filmer, which I described in *Lord Downshire And The United Irishmen*.

*

Fr. Patrick Dinneen, the strongest intellect and most stubborn character in the Irish Revival, knew of the poetry of Piers Ferriter from his youth in Slieve Luacra, where it had survived orally. In later life, after he had stopped functioning as a priest, he searched out manuscripts of Ferriter poems and gave them their first printed publication. Then, towards the end of his life, in 1929, he gave an account of his life in his popular booklet, *Four Notable Kerry Poets*. Extracts from that publication are given below:

"During the seventeenth and eighteenth centuries, to speak generally, the condition of the Irish was that of a tortured race, a race struggling desperately to keep themselves from extinction; struggling to maintain a foothold on the land that had nurtured them for tens of centuries; struggling to preserve some remnants not only of their national treasures, but also of their spiritual and intellectual possessions. They struggled for the land which reared them; for the churches and abbeys which their fathers built; for their native schools; for their native learning; for their literature and their ancient books. They struggled against enemies who greatly outnumbered them, who were unscrupulous in their aims and methods, hostile in their intellectual and spiritual outlook, and whose career of rapine seemed as inevitable as fate. The bulk of the population were dispossessed, and if still allowed to dwell in the lands of their fathers, it was as helots and wood-hewers. The churches and monasteries were confiscated and turned to alien uses. The clergy were scattered and their ministrations made criminal. Teachers were banned; schools were dispersed, and the office of teaching became punishable by law. A band of alien upstarts, lay and clerical, usurped the government of the country, and national life passed into the regions of romance. Native institutions were wiped out or had a precarious existence in shadows and fragments. The people, generation after generation, clinging to all that was dear to them, beheld the institutions in which they took pride sink below the horizon and leave them in a perilous and doubtful twilight. The first half of the eighteenth century would appear to be the darkest period of that national eclipse. The stamp of slavery was fast settling on the national character; the national virtues fostered in the light of freedom were becoming faint or obliterated; and it is a miracle of history that the bruised and broken race of that dark period should afterwards spring to their feet as a cohesive and resistless power.

"The remote and mountainous regions of the country were naturally the latest to be stripped of their national treasures, to be crushed and disorganised by superior force; and it is thus the modern county of Kerry with its moors and mountains was among the last regions in Ireland to have its share in the national institutions completely removed. The confiscation of property was likely to be less effective among hills and moors than in fertile plains. The right of assembly could be better vindicated under the shelter of overhanging hills; the crime of school-teaching could continue with a certain impunity where the school was a cabin in the recesses of impossible bogs, or even a sunlit fern-bank under the broad expanse of heaven.

"The struggle of these two centuries, a struggle not merely, perhaps not mainly, for material possessions but also for intellectual belongings and religious freedom, left its mark on the face of the country as well as on the character of the people. The country was shorn of its woods; the castles and mansions of the nobility were demolished or allowed to crumble into shapeless ruins and rarely did new buildings replace them; the abbeys and churches fell and tottered to decay; the industrious native population was elbowed to barren hillsides, while the choicest land was usurped by the stranger.

"The centuries in question undoubtedly left certain marks on the character of the people, and some of these marks were, of course, identical with those left by a régime of slavery on masses of population in every age of the world's history. But slavery, endured for several generations in the cause of Christian freedom and high intellectual ideals, is apt to engender compensating qualities...." (p1-2)

"Our ancestors, subdued by superior force, chanted their wrongs in the native speech attuned to native music. Those who were gifted among them with a genius for poetry, and especially for poetry wed to music, directed their poetic shafts against the oppressor, and in doing so illumined the darkness of the penal days as flashes of lightning illumine a murky sky. Their poetical effusions did much to lighten the burthen of oppression, to cheer those in bondage, and to turn wailing and sorrow into contentment and joy. The native language was a sort of musical instrument on which the skilled could play choice airs that lifted up the hearts of the people; now thrilling them with passion and resentment; now soothing them to contentment and resignation, and ever enkindling the hope of a speedy deliverance...." (p3)

"The singers and poets of this region of Ireland, those of them whose compositions have reached us, have had to be content with a local or provincial reputation owing to the deplorable conditions of Irish life, owing to the ban on intercommunication, on learning, on printing; but their ideal was not a region, a province, but an Ireland united and happy and independent. This ideal they gave expression to in dream and reverie, in simile, in song and lyric; they put no bounds to the Irish nation save the encircling sea.... They are local poets only through accidental causes. In more enlightened times, in times of free intercourse between Irishmen, of general printing, their memory will be cherished by all Irishmen at home and abroad...." (p6)

"...The furniture of their imagination, if the phrase be permissible, included legends and history not only of the Gaelic but also of the Anglo-Norman families; they seemed to see in the Ireland of the future a blend of Gaelic and Norman nobility, but their basic inspiration was Gaelic history and legend as well as Catholic tradition...." (p7)

"The four poets whom it is our privilege to honour represent in their active lives the greater part of two centuries of the life of the Irish nation. Pierce Ferriter represents the ancient chivalry of our nation, giving it perhaps a Norman flavour. He stands for all that is heroic in the history of our race. His heroism was tried and tested in a fiery furnace. He died for the faith that was in him. He had the courage to stand up against the Cromwellian horde who in their career through the land desecrated altars and murdered clerics. He defended his territory as long as mountain and morass combined with stout hearts and strong arms availed, and in the end laid down his life as a witness to his faith. He has left an example of heroism that enriches the annals of Irish chivalry; but his memory endures also as a sweet singer, one who in his lyrical effusions represents the refined and polished poetry of the middle ages; who made forms of verse that were rigid and exacting,breathing the very spirit of ancient chivalry. He composes with one eye on Irish character, Irish customs and manners, and another on the Catholic refinement and grace which distinguished the poetical literature of Europe in the Middle Ages. He comes before us with a twofold title to our veneration: as a chivalrous military chieftain who struggled vigorously against desperate odds and who laid down his life for the cause of truth, and as the sweet singer who enshrined in his Irish verse the concentrated essence of many ages of Christian chivalry. We honour him as a warrior, a martyr and a poet. He is one of the greatest heroes of the great century that produced him, of the great struggle in which he was overpowered, of the noble faith for which he died. He resisted at Tralee and elsewhere the forces of the Cromwellian parliament: leading in the fray picked men mainly from his own district of Duibhneacha. His life was cut short by treachery about 1653. Though nearly three hundred years have passed since he ruled in Ballyferriter, his memory is cherished to this day in his ancestral territory. The poet lamented in language of great dignity and beauty the Cromwellian transplantation and transportation decrees which affected rich and poor in Ireland...." (p13-14)

*

Ferriter is seen in a very different light by Mary Agnes Hickson, in her two-volume collection of Protestant documents from the 1640s and 1650s: *Ireland In The Seventeenth Century, Or, The Irish Massacres Of 1641-2*, published in London in 1884 with a Preface by James Anthony Froude. Mary Agnes Hickson was a Kerry historian in the same sense in which Field Marshal Kitchener, conqueror of the Sudan and Imperial War Minister in 1914, was a Kerry General. What appeared to her as the real Kerry were the small bodies of English Protestant planters put into the County a generation before 1641. The rest of Kerry, Norman and Gaelic, appeared to her as an untidy clutter left behind by untold ages of continuous living.

For Dinneen, the fact that people were absorbed in a way of life which countless generations of their ancestors had lived before them and that their highest aspiration was to live that life wholeheartedly in their own generation and transmit it to their children, was the best of reasons entitling them to do so. For Mary Agnes Hickson, it was the best of reasons for stopping them. What profit was there—what *progress* was there—in repeating yet again, for the purpose of mere contentment, such a well-established way of life?

Pierce Ferriter figures in two of the documents in her collection: in that of "Stephen Love, late of the town and parish of Killarney, in the barony of Magunihy, within the county of Kerry, a British Protestant" (CLXXXVII); and that of Michael Vines of Tralee, "shoemaker, a British Protestant" (CXXXVIII).

97

As the structures of the British state began to tear themselves apart in 1640-41, and the political framework of life went into flux, the recently expropriated Irish in many areas began to resume their property. At a certain moment, the little settlements of new English/Protestant conquerors in North Kerry withdrew from their various habitations into Tralee Castle. Then, "the English in the castle of Tralee, ...were besieged from the 14th of February, 1641, until the Christmas following" (Love). Among the besiegers was "Pierce Ferriter of Ferriter's Island, ...gentleman, then captain of a company". With him were Col. Donnel McCarthy, Capt. Florence MacFineen, Teigue MacDermot, Capt. Morris MacEligot, Walter Hussey, etc.

In the course of the siege, "this deponent likewise saith, that he heard Captain Pierse Ferriter and other rebels did say, that they had the King's Commission for what they did, and therewithal he sent a copy of the same into the warders of the said castle, and said that we were the rebels and those (with him)... the king's subjects". (Vines. "1641" here was 1642 by our reckoning. For some reason which I forget, the year at that time did not change until the Spring, and January and part of February belonged to the previous year. One sometimes sees the year written as, for example, "January 1641/2".)

In the circumstances of the time, Ferriter's claim to be acting on behalf of the Crown was at least as good as the claim of those in Tralee Castle to be doing so. That is why I refer to the 1641 affair as "a so-called rebellion" on the Irish side. The orderly structure of the state had been broken down by events in England, and there was no longer an agreed source of authority. And, if there is no authoritative structure of state, how can there be a rebellion against it? Insofar as the word "rebellion" can be meaningfully applied to an understanding of the events of the 1640s, it is as Lord Clarendon applied it in his incomparable history of the English Civil War as *The Great Rebellion*: that is to say, as the rebellion of a faction of political incompetents in the English Parliament against the established form of government.

Events in Ireland were precipitated by the breakdown of the English state and its Irish administration. In that situation, the different social fragments in Ireland were left to tend to their affairs as best they could in a political vacuum. In North Kerry the recent English planters withdrew into Tralee Castle and were put under siege by the natives, i.e., the Old Irish and the Normans who had become more Irish than the Irish. The siege was resolved peacefully: "He also saith, that the castle was yielded upon quarter for their lives, and a suit of clothes a piece" (Vines).

Vines also deposed that a number of people "who before this rebellion were Protestants, have since turned Papists, and go under the rebel's colours and do fight for the rebels against the English".

Four names are given in this connection: Bradfield, MacMorrish, O'Lenane, and McMurrough. It would be a fair guess that the latter three had declared themselves Protestants under strong inducements from the state, and that the effective dissolution of the state ended their reason for being Protestant. And if

Bradfield had taken a liking for the Irish way of life, or had begun to feel dubious about the life of a planted conqueror, why should he not have become a Papist on the basis of human affinity? It was through the logic of the Reformation state in England, and especially of its Parliamentary dimension, that a strict identity was made between religion and nationality.

Document CXC in Mary Agnes Hickson's collection is by "William Dethick, late of Killvallehagh (*recte* Killballylahiff), in the parish of Killiny in the barony of Corcaguiny, within the county of Kerry, gent. a British Protestant". Dethick swore:

> "that about the last of January, 1641, and since the beginning of the present rebellion, he lost, was robbed, and was forcibly despoiled of his goods and chattels of 402*l*. 10*s*. [£402.50]. Also he saith, that his ... goods were taken... by Walter Hussey of Castle Gregory... gent., Owen MacMoriarty of Castle Drum, gent., Owen MacDonnel Oge of Keelgarrylander... in the said barony, gent., and their associates to the number of a hundred men in hostile manner. He also said that his ammunition, viz. one of his guns, was taken away by Owen MacDonnell Oge aforesaid, and another of his guns was taken away by the captains and commanders at the siege of Tralee... He also saith, that the persons above mentioned who took away his goods were they who robbed most of the Protestants in that part of the barony aforesaid, ...about the time aforesaid".

Dethick further deposed that sixteen Protestants in Killarney who had failed to find refuge in a Castle "were taken by the MacCarthys and their followers in those parts, and being stripped, were first whipped up and down from one side of the town to the other, and a great hole being made for the purpose, they were thrown into it, and so buried alive. This the deponent saw not with his own eyes, but he dares avouch it for truth, because he hath heard it most confidently related from the mouths of many Protestants". The remainder of the deposition consists of remarks on the siege of Tralee Castle.

Mary Agnes Hickson is stimulated to moral reflection in a Note to this document:

> "This deponent was probably the son of Humphrey Dethick, one of the first twelve free burgesses of Tralee named in the charter granted 31st of March, 1611, Robert Blennerhassett being provost. Humphrey Dethick was also the latter's colleague in the representation of the borough in 1613. I have in the above deposition, as in the former ones, omitted the long inventory of lost goods, lands, &c, and their money value. Amongst them salt works carried on in Killballylahiff and tucking mills there are mentioned, showing how the son of the M.P. for Tralee did not disdain trade, and how the industrial resources of even the most remote districts in the west of Ireland were being utilised by the colonists until the land was once more reduced to a waste by an ill-advised rebellion. A curious proof of the dislike of the Irish to mercantile pursuits is furnished in the... Irish poem by Pierce Ferriter, the rebel leader, translated for

the Percy Society by Crofton Croker. Describing the wailing of the *banshee* or guardian spirit for Maurice FitzGerald, son of the Knight of Kerry, who died on the eve of the rebellion, Ferriter says:—

> The prosperous traders
> Were filled with affright,
> In Tralee they packed up
> And made ready for flight,
>
> For there a shrill voice
> At the door of each hall
> Was heard, as they fancied,
> Regretting *their* fall.
>
> They fled to concealment,
> Ah! fools thus to fly—
> For no trader a Banshee
> Would utter a cry!

"Acting out what he wrote, Ferriter marched with his Hussey and Geraldine associates to Tralee, sweeping poor Mr. Dethick's salt pans and tucking mills into the sea and the rivers, and leaving the districts of Castle Gregory and Killballylahiff in a state of desolation and poverty, from which they have never thoroughly recovered to this day." (p118-9)

*

It should be evident that we are here on the delicate ground of genocide. Some English authorities of the early 17th century, when reviewing the history of English rule in Ireland, came to the conclusion that the extermination of the Irish was logically implicit in it throughout. Maybe so. But, if so, the genocide project was effectively obstructed by the way so many of the early colonists behaved as Normans rather than English, and took to being Irish themselves, and it was delayed by the preoccupation of the English state with wars in France and dynastic civil wars in England. It is only with the establishment of the Reformation state in England that the genocide project in Ireland became explicit, and was taken in hand with a will.

The '1641 Rebellion' was an interruption of the English genocide project. Some lost ground was recovered. Lands were taken back and other forms of Plantation property confiscated. Some planters were killed in the process, but no general agreement as to approximate numbers has ever been reached.

I was living in Belfast when I made a brief excursion into this numbers game in the 1970s. There was no better time or place for doing it, because the spirit of 1641 was the contemporary spirit of Belfast in the early 1970s. And I think there was no better position from which to do it than the curious position I held in political life in Belfast then—I was a Munster Catholic (unbelieving, but for all practical purpose as much a Catholic to Protestant eyes as if I had been a daily communicant), but I was preoccupied with the history of Protestant Ulster. And, because I was using every opportunity to try to convey to nationalist Ireland my insight that the Ulster Protestants would not behave under pressure as they were expected to behave, I was caricatured as a kind of Orange bigot by the middle class press in Dublin (which was then far removed from its present 'Dublin 4' outlook). What I got to understand very quickly from that viewpoint was how little factual detail mattered to the Protestant understanding of events involving Catholics.

The '1641 Rebellion' was a rebellion, even though there was no established authority for it to overthrow, because it was an affront to Providence, to a self-evident destiny. And it mattered not at all whether there was an active native counter-genocide to the English genocide project in Ireland—the stopping of the civilising English genocide was in itself an outrage, an affront to destiny.

There has been in English political culture since the strange English Reformation a conviction that England is the manifestation of a force of destiny in the life of the world. It is an entirely unreflecting and uncritical conviction, less subject to reason than any 'Papist' dogma, and it has displayed an extraordinary power to motivate participants in the English state to engage in destructive tampering with the lives of others. Its devotees are in the grip of a feeling that some great purpose in the life of the universe will be thwarted, that destiny will fail and cosmic catastrophe ensue, if this particular people, or that one, is not prevented from continuing to live as it has lived for a thousand years. Long-established ways of life must be broken up, if necessary by the extermination of the people who are stubbornly intent on continuing to live them, for the purpose of ensuring that they do not obstruct the progression of progress towards its end.

But what is the end of progress? It has no end, because if it ended, it would no longer be progress, and it is unthinkable that there should not be progress. There must therefore be endless progress in which the over-riding purpose at any given moment is to break up stable ways of life in which people are living more or less contentedly.

In the historic relationship between England and Ireland, progress has meant the expansion of the English people at the expense of the Irish under the hegemony of the English state. And the values which are objectified as destiny and are held to justify English conduct, are generalisations of the strong points which enabled the English to progress at the expense of the Irish, and to see extermination of the Irish as a realistic and moral project.

If we accept the English position on this delicate matter, but at the same time retain our critical faculties, we are led to the conclusion that there are two kinds of genocide, which have entirely different moral values. Good genocide is a cost of progress. It is what the English state attempted with partial success in Ireland over many centuries, and achieved with complete success in other Continents. Genocide which is not a cost of progress is reprehensible.

This is the unarticulated English view of the matter. Applied to 1641, it led to the fierce denunciation of the interruption by Ferriter and his associates all around the country of the progressive, civilising genocide which had been in process since late Elizabethan times. And any planter who was killed in the accomplishing of that interruption was the victim of reactionary genocide.

*

The break-down of the English state as an actual and authoritative administration was the precipitating cause of social conflict within Ireland in 1641. Religious difference was the general medium of the conflict.

But religious difference was not merely the difference between Protestantism in England and Catholicism in Ireland. Indeed, the Protestant/Catholic difference would have been of little practical political account if Protestant England had known what it was. The deadly matter for Ireland was that it got caught between the factions of English Protestantism, which were also factions of the English state.

Ireland was 'loyal' and peaceful in 1640 under the Government of Thomas Wentworth, Lord Strafford.

England, since its Reformation, had been above all else a state—not a people, nor a nation, nor a 'tradition', but a state. In other kinds of society 'loyalty' might have other grounds, but in a society which is above all else a state, 'loyalty' is to a considerable extent a function of stable, regular and consistent administration. And, by the same token, if a state which is the active organiser of society breaks down, the social peace which depended on the regular functioning of that state will tend to break down with it. I saw that happen at close quarters in Northern Ireland following the events of August 1969. And it is what happened in 1641.

Strafford had governed the country with an unprecedented regularity from 1633 to 1640 and the country was peaceful. Early in 1641 he was executed (one might even say assassinated) by the English Parliament, and all that he had constructed in Ireland fell apart.

Although Strafford's government of Ireland figured largely in the charges brought against him, what he was executed for was what he represented in English political life. And English political life was shot through with religious conflict— conflict within Protestantism resulting from the unreligious source of its religious Reformation.

The part played by religion in the life of native Irish society was essentially different from the part played by religion in the life of the English state. The Irish were not religiously aggressive. When Irish Christian missionaries went out to Britain and Europe in the Dark Ages, they went as preachers and exemplars, entirely unsupported by military force. But the English state from the time of the Conquest onwards was a crusading state in which the secular and the sacred marched together. William the Conqueror acted as a secular arm of the revolutionary Papacy of the eleventh century. His great-grandson, Henry II, was commissioned by the Pope to take Ireland in hand and bring it within the discipline of the Roman Church. And Henry VIII had his mind set on a Crusade against Lutheranism, and had been named Defender of the Faith by the Pope, when for reasons of state he enacted his breach with Rome.

At the moment of the English Reformation, the English state had for three and a half centuries been the force holding Ireland in connection with Rome. Then, when it broke with Rome, it required that the Irish should do likewise.

Twenty-five years ago, I published a booklet with the title, *The Rise Of Papal Power In Ireland*, in which I argued that native Ireland did not become 'Papist' in its doctrine and organisation until the mid-19th century—until it had been demoralised by the Famine and made simple by the loss of its language, and was thus in a suitable condition to be taken in hand by Cardinal Cullen and remade in strict accordance with the decrees adopted by the Council of Trent three hundred years earlier. Perhaps I exaggerated a bit, but I do not think that I exaggerated much. I suggested that the intensity of the strict Roman regime in Irish life from the 1850s to the 1970s could not possibly have prevailed throughout the millennium and a half since St. Patrick. Its intensity and simplicity were signs of its novelty.

If modern Catholicism in Ireland had grown out of the traditional Christianity of Gaelic Ireland, it would have been similar in many respects to the old Catholicism of countries like Spain and Germany. But it was startlingly unlike the Catholicism of those countries.

My argument was not well received a quarter of a century ago, but much that has happened since then tends to bear it out. And I notice that Fr. J.J. O'Riordan of Kiskeam (who is I believe a cousin of mine) has remarked on the singularity of the "Catholicism *du type Irelandais*" created by Cardinal Cullen (*Irish Catholics—Tradition And Transition,* Veritas 1980).

Henry II was commissioned by the Pope to make Christianity in Ireland strictly Roman in its discipline. But, throughout the following centuries, the Roman ecclesiastical discipline tended to be confined to areas of Norman and Viking settlement. When Henry VIII demanded that the Irish should break with Rome, they had as yet formed only the loosest attachment to Rome.

Irish Christianity was not theocratic. It had an honoured place within the traditional culture of native Ireland, but it did not have a position of dominance over the other elements of social culture. Neither was it theological in its preoccupations. The Church hierarchy benevolently acknowledged the supremacy of Rome, but it did not stand on independent ground from which it might have gained leverage against the other elements of the traditional culture, even though that was the Roman system. And, in its devotional and ideological life, it did not strive for a totalitarian theology through which social life would be subordinated to some purpose beyond itself.

The relationship between Gaelic Ireland and its Christian and pagan saints and heroes—the character of its idolatry, as a Protestant theocrat would put it—might be compared to the relationship between ancient Athens and its goddess, Athena, as described by Hegel:

"Athena is the town of Athens, and is also the spirit of the particular Athenian people; not an external spirit or protecting spirit, but the spirit which is actually alive in the people... The knowledge the subject has of the gods is not a

103

knowledge of them merely as abstractions beyond the sphere of reality. It is a knowledge of the concrete subjectivity of man himself as something essential, for the gods are within him. Here we have not that negative relation, where the relation of the subject to what is above him... is the sacrifice of its consciousness. The powers here are friendly and gracious to men, they dwell in man's own breast; man gives them reality, and knows their reality to be at the same time his own. The breath of freedom pervades this whole world, and constitutes the fundamental principle for this attitude of mind" (*Lectures On The Philosophy Of Religion.* Translated from the 1901 Leiden edition, p507).

Between this culture and the frantically theological Protestantism of England there was no common ground.

*

English Protestantism did not arise out of any issue of religious principle, and it was not in origin a religious movement at all. Difference over religion was not the cause of its breach with Rome, but a consequence of it. The break with Rome happened for a very narrow and specific reason of state. The King needed a divorce because his wife of 20 years, Catherine of Aragon, had proved unable to produce a son with him, and he needed a male heir to secure an orderly succession to the throne. The monarchy had gone through a very long period of internal dynastic dispute and civil war, from which it had emerged only with the accession of the King's father, Henry VII. Under these Tudor Kings, England had become one of the great powers of Europe. There was, however, a possibility of relapse into dynastic civil war if the succession to Henry VIII was disputable. Henry therefore had sound reasons of state for needing a son born in holy wedlock, and he applied to the Pope for a divorce.

The Papacy was then an integral part of the political order of western Europe, performing functions of mediation and facilitation. The overlapping of the spheres of Church and State was taken for granted by all concerned, and it was the acknowledged role of the Papacy to use its ultimate spiritual authority to relieve difficulties in practical life that a strict application of religious principle might be causing.

Pope Leo XIII would certainly have seen it as his duty to relieve the English state from the danger caused by the lack of a royal son, and would have granted the King a divorce from Catherine, if another state had not intervened to prevent him.

The Emperor Henry V, the successor of Charlemagne, the Holy Roman Emperor, was the most powerful monarch in Europe. He was the nephew of Henry's wife. He was already in conflict with the Pope and was pressing down on Rome. And he absolutely forbade the Pope to divorce his aunt. And therein lies the origin of the English Reformation.

Henry was in a hurry and so he divorced himself. But he did not divorce himself by transferring the institution of marriage to the sphere of purely secular law. What he did was constitute himself his own Pope by declaring himself head of the Church in England.

It was not his intention that England should be made Protestant. He did not aspire to subvert the Faith of which he had been named Defender. But, once he had acted as his own Pope in order to grant himself a divorce, one thing led to another. By the end of his reign, a kind of incoherent Protestantism had been established piecemeal through the action of his state. Popular institutions through which the populace was connected with Rome had been abolished. Extensive Church properties had been confiscated and sold off to a new gentrifying middle class. The country had been directed into total antagonism with Rome. But Henry kept on changing his mind as to what the new religion of England was to be, and so England knew what it was not, but did not yet know what it was.

Henry's young son (by Jane Seymour), Edward VI, proclaimed a systematic Protestantism, but he died before it could achieve stability as a structure of state. His half-sister, Mary (Henry's daughter by Catherine of Aragon), restored the old Catholic religion, but her reign was as brief as Edward's (six years each). Then came Elizabeth (Henry's daughter by Anne Boleyn), with a reign of 45 years but an equivocating attitude towards the religion of the Church of which she was head.

The complacency with which such a large section of the English people, at the behest of the King, discarded the religion of their ancestors—and the religion in which they themselves had lived contentedly until the moment when the King issued his instructions—and the willingness with which they went over to a new religion which had no definite form as yet, would suggest that they had little concern with religious matters, and that they were above all else members of a state.

The breach with Rome had the effect of making the English state absolute in its pretensions, by removing it from the system of European states, and by abolishing the Church/State division internally.

The primary role accorded to the Papacy in European diplomacy was not an imposition of military power, but a convenience of international relations between states that shared a common origin and functioned within a common system of values. And the distinction of the internal life into the spheres of Church and State was one of the distinctive features of European life. With the displacement of the Pope by the King as head of the Church, the English state asserted absolute authority over all social life, sacred as well as secular. The Church/State division was abolished. Religious uniformity was established by political decree. And England confronted Europe and the world as an absolute state, acknowledging no limit on its power other than the reach of that power, and acknowledging no morality other than the rule that whatever helped it to extend its power was right.

It appeared for a couple of generations following the break with Rome that the power-politics of the break was sufficient ideological ground for it, and that the *ad hoc*, fluctuating nature of the new religion was entirely adequate to its function in English life. But then, in the late Elizabethan period, England went theological, and for the next two or three centuries it was the most fertile producer of theological material in the world. The loss of theological certainty, consequent on the break with Rome and Henry's indecisiveness when it came to laying down a dogmatic structure for his new Church, began to rankle. A profound yearning to reach theological certainty arose. Theological disputations built up to a frenzy. Religious sects were formed. A movement towards the formation of a strictly theocratic state set in.

All of this might be summed up as Puritanism. But, although it can be given a single name, it did not have substantial uniformity of belief and purpose. Theological dispute did not tend towards agreement. The more subtle it became, the more it opened up the range of possible disagreement. And the more the potential for disagreement was opened up, the more it became the case that the only substantial point of agreement between all parties was anti-Catholicism. Tirades against Papism and Papists therefore took on a life of their own, unrelated to any actual threat to the independence of Protestant England from France or Spain. Anti-Papist hysteria became necessary to the internal life of England as a point of unity for its welter of centrifugal theological tendencies, and it was still in full flow two centuries after 1641, when England had become indisputably the dominant military power in the world.

In 1641 the Puritans, who were the most vehement of the anti-Papists, were poised for a seizure of political power in England. They dominated Parliament, and were disputing state authority with the King, with the result that the state as an administration operating under a generally agreed system of authority, ceased to function. And the first decisive exercise of power by Parliament was the killing of Strafford (Wentworth), the King's Irish Deputy since 1633, under whose administration Ireland had been at peace.

*

No Parliament had been held in England between 1628 and 1640. Strafford, who was killed on trumped-up charges after a rigged trial in May 1641, had been the leader of Parliament in 1628. He had changed sides then after failing to persuade his Parliamentary colleagues that there was a dimension of discretionary power involved in the governing of states which they were not allowing for. As he saw it, Parliament was acting on an inadequate understanding of state affairs, one which would only have enabled it to disable the process of government. He therefore went into the service of the King with the object of enabling him to govern as far as possible without calling Parliaments to vote subsidies. He did this by imposing a regularity of administration, with a view to maximising revenues from regular sources.

His first office was President of the North, meaning the North of England, which was then governed in two parts. Then, in 1633, he took on the Government of Ireland as an additional office. In both offices he succeeded in increasing revenue by regularity of administration. In Ireland he also called Parliaments which voted subsidies.

I would say that, by the only standards which it is sensible to apply, given the general framework of things, Strafford governed Ireland extraordinarily well.

One of the charges in his impeachment was that he described Ireland as "a conquered country", and governed it as such. Outrage at this way of describing Ireland was expressed by the very English Parliament which nine years later authorised the Cromwellian regime of terror in Ireland.

The charge was true. Strafford governed Ireland as a conquered country, and governed it well. But Ireland was never actually governed as anything but a conquered country.

Mary Agnes Hickson works up great indignation against Strafford, because of: "...his fixed idea, to which he held fast even at his trial in Westminster Hall, being that Ireland was a conquered country, to be governed solely by and for the pleasure of the King. With his mind filled with this dangerous half-truth, he set himself the task of outwitting and browbeating the Lords Justices, forgetting in his arrogance that they were natives of the conquering country, and one of them, a veteran in political intrigues, as as able and as strong-willed as himself, and understood the spirit of the times far better than he did. Wentworth, with all the advantages of his position as a royal favourite, was no match for '*Old Richard*' as ...he calls the Earl of Cork, who, before his enemy was born, had foiled the great ones at Elizabeth's council board" (Vol. 1, p53).

Strafford did not govern as a kind of feudal chairman, negotiating with Richard Boyle, Earl of Cork, grandee of the Munster Plantation, and the other grandees who felt they were entitled to be absolute masters in their own extensive domains and that they were subjects of the Crown only by way of make-believe. Therefore, Mary Agnes Hickson concludes, "from the Giant's Causeway to Cape Clear the island was like a volcano on the eve of an eruption, and Wentworth had not a dozen friends left in the council and the country" (Vol. 1, p69).

That the grandees detested Strafford because he treated them as subjects there is no doubt. And it was not nice for Lord Cork to be compelled to disgorge stolen property, and to pay fines just as if he was one of the multitudes of nobodies over whom he himself exercised power. People who are not used to being governed do not like it when government takes them in hand. Nevertheless, even though powerful people on all sides were offended by Strafford's administration, he was always able to call Parliaments which gave him what he wanted.

And his Parliaments were representative to a very considerable degree. Indeed, the complaint was made against one of his Parliaments, that it operated a "divide and rule" strategy by having a representation that was 50/50 Protestant and Catholic (or 49/49 with a 2% makeweight of his own nominees). That is not a complaint that it was ever again possible to make against a Viceroy. Division arising from equality of representation in the Parliament of the Kingdom of Ireland, operating under the authority of an independent Crown, was replaced by a very different kind of division, under which Cathoics were simply excluded from representation in an Irish Parliament which was only a devolved institution of the English Parliament, with the Crown reduced to the status of a facade on the English Parliament.

*

To discuss whether Strafford's Irish regime was just in some general way related to Irish purposes would be to enter the realm of fantasy. Justice in that sense had nothing to do with the Strafford regime, any more than with the English regimes that preceded him for hundreds of years, or with the English regimes that succeeded him for hundreds of years.

The good government of Ireland considered as an end in itself was never an object of English policy. It was not even a possible object of English policy. In the realm of statecraft, Ireland existed for English purposes. Very often all that was required was that Ireland should be kept harmless as an appendage of the English state—but keeping it harmless to England was not the same thing as not inflicting harm on Ireland. Strafford, however, engaged in positive, constructive government in Ireland, although for an English purpose of state.

One might even say Strafford governed Ireland for a British purpose of state because, on the death of Elizabeth, the King of Scotland had become the King of England too, and Gaelic Ireland was able to find in its traditions a basis for attachment to the Stuart monarchy. But his purpose was, of course, predominantly English, if only because England was the main substance of the monarchy of the Three Kingdoms. And his purpose in governing Ireland well was to make it a secure foundation for the monarchical state against the subversive tendencies of the English Parliament.

But, granted that his purposes were English, and regardless of the merits of the Crown versus Parliament argument in England, it should be acknowledged that what he attempted to do was more conducive to good government in Ireland than any possible alternative. Ireland was held in secure subjection to England and there was nothing to be done about that. The constitutional form of the subjection was through the monarchy. There was notionally a dual monarchy under the one Crown. The possibility that Ireland might be governed to some extent as a distinct kingdom, and not be continually tampered with in the service of particular English interests, lay with the monarchy as an actual governing force in the state, drawing strength from its Three Kingdoms, and preventing the English Parliament from going beyond its traditional role and usurping the power of government.

Strafford formed a distinct Irish administration for the King—administrative, judicial, and commercial. He enhanced the role of administrative law in order to give law more general effect and make it something better than a playground for the grandees. He tried to make the legal system in Ireland autonomous by banning appeals by the grandees to the English Privy Council against judgments given against them in Ireland. And he fostered commercial developments in Ireland.

The rise of the English Parliament to dominance in the state begins with the Parliamentary killing of Strafford, although it took a further three-quarters of a century to establish the Parliamentary regime securely and reduce the Crown to a Parliamentary rubber stamp. It has become customary to equate the rise of Parliamentary power in the state with the establishment of democracy, but there is no basis in historical fact for that equation. Parliamentary rule was for many generations the rule of an aristocratic oligarchy with extensive commercial interests, and it ensured that Ireland was governed in strict subordination to English commercial interests, and in accordance with the anti-Papist mania of the powreful, but internally divided and insecure Protestantism of England.

English history is propaganda written in support of the victorious political order. It is therefore strongly Parliamentary in its bias. And, after the democratisation of Parliament in the late 19th century or the early 20th century (depending on how extensive a franchise is considered necessary for democracy), a democratic dimension was projected backwards to the long era when Parliament was entirely undemocratic, both in structure and principle. The Strafford of real life all but disappears from view beneath all those layers of intensively elaborated ideology or propaganda.

C.H. Firth was one of the better middle class 17th century historians of late 19th century England. He supplied an Introduction to the *Life Of Strafford* written by Robert Browning, the poet, in the 1830s, and published by The Browning Society in 1892, in which he wrote:

"In the spring of 1640, when Strafford left Ireland, it seemed as if his purpose had been attained. 'This people', he writes, 'is abundantly comforted and satisfied with your justice [i.e., the King's justice], set with exceeding alacrity to serve the crown the right way in these doubtful times...'

"Yet all this appearance of success was delusive. Strafford's work failed to endure, and its failure was in part due to his own errors. In his desire to realise his conception of good government as rapidly as possible he had regarded all means as legitimate. His severity had alienated the nobles and officials who had hitherto formed the governing class in Ireland. Presbyterian and Puritan colonists had been driven into opposition by his determination to enforce a conformity to the Anglican Church. His plantations of Clare and Ormond, and his intended plantation of Connaught, had roused the fears of the native Irish for their lands. The meeting of the Long Parliament set free all these different resentments and destroyed the strong government he had set up. A year later the outbreak of the Irish rebellion caused largely by Strafford's agrarian policy, swept away the material prosperity he had created. But even with 20 years of absolute power, he could hardly have effected what he sought to do in six or seven, for he relied upon force to effect social changes which force alone was insufficient to accomplish, and left out of account the necessity of obtaining the co-operation of the people he governed."

In fact, Strafford's use of force was minimal by comparison with what went before him and what came after him. It was an orderly power of state directed against the grandees whom he held to terms which they had once agreed to but had long since broken.

He had of course a plantation policy. Plantation was fundamental to English policy in Ireland. As Francis Bacon put it in a ceremonial speech as Keeper of the Great Seal in 1717:

"Ireland is the last *exfiliis Europae* which hath been reclaimed from desolation

109

and a desert (in many parts) to population and plantation; and from savage barbarous customs to humanity and civility. This is the King's work in chief. It is his garland of heroical virtue and felicity, denied to his progenitors and reserved to his times" (James Spedding, *Life And Times Of Francis Bacon*. 1878, p218).

So Strafford had a plantation scheme as a matter of course. And he intended to make a comprehensive resettlement of Connaught, establishing as far as possible communities of farmers, of Irish as well as English stock, as social support for monarchy.

But he was also considering the uprooting of a Plantation—the one that has been the source of endless trouble, but which was admired above all others by Mary Agnes Hickson. All the other plantations 'took', in the sense that a merging of peoples happened on them in the long run. The Plantation of Ulster alone did not take.

*

The trouble for Strafford began with the war between England and Scotland over religion (what else!). It was to finance this war that the King called an English Parliament in 1640. The Puritans were taken by surprise, the war against the Scots was popular, and Parliament voted the money and was disbanded. But the King handled affairs badly and had to call another Parliament later in 1640. The Puritans were ready this time, and they carried the representation in what might be fairly called the first party election campaign in English history.

When the Anglo-Scottish conflict erupted, Strafford had to consider what the Ulster Plantation was in that context. Had the Scots in Ulster become Irish? Was their allegiance to the Kingdom in which they had been given land at the expense of the natives? Or were they, as we would put it nowadays, a Fifth Column acting in the Scottish interest outside the Kingdom of Scotland?

Strafford required them to acknowledge that they were subjects of the King in his capacity as King of Ireland, and that Scottish affairs were no longer their business. The Oath, by means of which they were required to make this acknowledgement, was regarded as an outrage on their liberty by the Presbyterians, and was known as the Black Oath. Strafford therefore considered whether the Plantation of Ulster, in its Scottish dimension, should be written off as a failure, and whether remedial measures should be taken while the Army which had been raised for the emergency was available.

In a note written in August 1640, he considers, "Whether as the condition of affairs now stand in the three kingdoms, it bee of absolute necessity for the publique sauftie of this kingdom, and for securing it from Scottish invasion, to banish all the under Scots in Ulster by proclamation, grounded upon an humble request of the Co'mons House in this p'nte P'liamt".

He discusses the matter as follows:

"Distinction should be put between the under Scotts, who are soe numerous and soe ready for insurrecc'on; and such as have considerable estates in lands,

110

to ingage and secure fidelities. It will alsoe be of use to declare it a conditionall banishment till peace bee firmly settled.

"Happly it will be objected, that the Scots in Ulster took the oath administered in implicit abjuration of the covenant, that they are the Kings subjects, not yet convinced of actuall rebellion. That it will bee a hard case to banishe the Kinge's people upon supposition and conjecture; and that by this course the major parte of all the North will bee untenanted.

"To this I answer, that mainie thousands in the Northe never tooke the oathe; and as I am certainely made believe, they now publiquely avouch it as an unlawful oath; and for ought I see, they will shortly retourne, to any that dares question them, such an answere as Rob't Bruce, Earle of Carricke, made to Sir John Comyn, whoe, chargeing him with breach of oath taken at Westminster to King Edward, replyes with cleaving Sir John's head in twoe... None is soe dim-sighted but sees the gen'all inclination of the Ulster Scots to the Covenant; and God forbid they should tarrie there till the Earle of Argile brings them armies to cut our throats... And what Co'mon wealth will not give waie that a few landlords (and they are but a few) should receive some small p'judice, where the publique sauftie and certaine peace of the whole is concerned.

"It will be objected that the Scots are manie in number, evrie ordinarie fellow still carrieing his sword and pistoll; and therefore unsaufe to bee too farr provoaked. I answer, 'tis more unsaufe to deale with an enemy by hauves; and that I feare will fall out to bee our case if resolutely this designe bee not put in execuc'on; for whoe sees not if the now standing army bee not able, wth out anie manner of daunger or difficultie, to give them the lawe, and send them forthwith pacqueing—I say, who sees not that (upon Argile's landing and armeing them) we shall be exposed to a most assured scorne and certaine ruine? What number of boats and barques will serve for the transportac'on and passage of soe manie, how they maie be suddainly and without noyse provided, and in what havens they should be loaded from Argiles reach... prop' for p'sonall debate with such as are acquainted in those partes" (*The Life And Original Correspondence Of Sir George Radcliffe*, edited by T.D. Whitaker, 1810, p208-10. Radcliffe was related by marriage to Strafford, and acted in his Irish administration).

Strafford's watchword was "Thorough". It is impressive proof of his thoroughness that he identified this major flaw in the social composition in Ireland and had it in mind to do something about it.

Of course, nothing came of it. He was arrested by the English Parliament a couple of months later, given a show trial, to which the Irish grandees he had offended contributed, and he was executed. And then things flew apart.

*

When Firth writes, "Strafford's work failed to endure, and its failure was in part due to his own errors", his reasoning is in substance that the failure to endure is proof of its errors. But there is no need for circular reasoning here, because the causes of failure are plain. Parliament undermined the state structure within which Strafford had pulled things together, and therefore things fell apart.

The English state had constructed Ireland into a social patchwork during the couple of generations prior to 1640. There could be no spontaneous sense of community between those patches, some of which had just got off the boat. They could be drawn together into the semblance of a general body politic only by the purposeful pressure of the state on all of them. The easy way of government would be through alliance with the more powerful grandees, leaving them to hold down the rest. Strafford was more ambitious. He wanted to develop Ireland into a secure base of monarchy, therefore he established Crown government independent of the grandees and, by treating all as subjects, made none feel excluded. If the monarchy had survived, perhaps the patchwork would have developed a sense of community and become a body politic, as a consequence of this kind of government continued over a number of generations. As it was, the monarchy fell, and with it the established administration of state, there was a long gap in which there was no legitimate political order, the rising power of Parliament was on an extravagant anti-Papist binge in alliance with the Plantation Scots in Ireland, and things flew apart.

A state cannot fall apart and things remain otherwise as they had been.

The British state apparatus of Northern Ireland went berserk for a week in August 1969. A year earlier, it was widely agreed that relations between the two Northern communities had never been better. The activity of the state in that week in August set them at one another's throats.

Yugoslavia is another case in point. The three national communities in Bosnia had developed such close relations in the framework of the Yugoslav state that they were regarded as having ceased to be distinct communities at all. Then the component territories of the Yugoslav state were pulled apart with the active encouragement of Germany and Britain (which was its architect), and the three national communities restored themselves with remarkable speed and reverted to the traditional Balkan mode of communal relations.

Relations between the half dozen major social components of the Irish patchwork in 1640 were nowhere near as amicable as Bosnian relations in 1988, and there is accordingly much less ground for surprise at what happened when the state framework in which they were held together fell apart. But I know of only one writer who has seen things in this light:

"On the collapse of the Monarchy Ireland split up into half a dozen embryo States."

"One has only to give the Government of these islands a tiny shock and withdraw the police from one city to get a repetition of what occurred in Ulster in 1641."

"When Strafford left Ireland all was at peace. For the year that intervened between his departure and his fall, despite disaster after disaster that fell on the King's party, not a murmur came from the North. All the rest of Ireland remained loyal. It was not till after his fall that the elements began to stir. They stirred because every detail of his administration was reversed."

"One can understand what occurred in Ulster when the news went round that Scotland had carried a successful rebellion. England was in revolt, the army was demoralised, the lands and goods of the planters were fair game."

Those observations are from a two-volume work, *Strafford in Ireland*, by Hugh O'Grady. It was published in Dublin in 1923, which was not the best time to have notice taken of it.

*

When the established order in a state breaks down, and the component parts of the state apparatus make war on each other, how is 'loyalty' possible? What is there to be 'loyal' to? There is no established structure of legitimacy through which a desire to be loyal could be safely accomplished.

Loyalty could not even be accomplished by picking the ultimate winner at the start and sticking to him throughout, because the terms of the conflict were not set at the start and adhered to until one side won out. The alignment of parties kept changing through the 1640s, as did the issues.

One hears it said that Cromwell brought Republicanism to Ireland. In fact, Cromwell was not a Republican at all.If the issue in England had been between Parliamentary Republicanism and Monarchism, it would have been resolved in favour of the Republic within a few years. But Parliament was not Republican. Even though it rebelled against the Crown, it still claimed to be acting on the authority of the Crown. It had no realisable objective of its own—unless it was the Presbyterian scheme for a Covenanted theocracy with the King at its head. The English Parliament at one point voted for the Covenant, but Charles I didn't see himself as King in a Puritan theocracy. After his death Charles II, in flight from the English, became the Covenanted King in Scotland, but Cromwell put an end to that.

Charles I was executed by the English Parliament in January 1649. But he was not executed for the purpose of establishing a Republic. He was executed because Parliament could see no other way of bringing its rebellion to a conclusive success. The Republic was merely the *de facto* consequence of the execution of the King. There was extensive popular support for monarchy, and therefore Parliament, no matter how many battles it won, could never rest easy as long as there was a King in England. But the Cromwellians had to purge Parliament of its major constituent, the Presbyterians, before they could get it to authorise the killing of the King.

The Presbyterians, who had set off the whole thing by rebelling against the King, now rebelled against Parliament and hailed the executed King's son as Charles II. The Ulster Presbyterians put the Cromwellian force in Derry under siege. Their siege was broken by Owen Roe O'Neill's army of the Ulster clans, which had formed an alliance with the Cromwellian English Parliament. O'Neill was feted by the Cromwellians in Derry a few weeks before the English Parliament repudiated the Treaty with him, and the Cromwellian conquest was launched.

Where does one find a ground of 'loyalty' in all of that? Cromwell defeated his former Scots allies in battle, established his regime of terror in Ireland, and established a unitary state across both islands. It was a state without a King, and was therefore a Republic. But it did not know how to be a republic. It was governed as a military dictatorship by Cromwell.

Soon after peace was restored (which is to say, soon after the regime of terror was securely established in Ireland), the existential problems of the 'Commonwealth' began, and the proposal was made that the only possible solution was for Cromwell to found a new monarchy. Cromwell gave serious thought to becoming King Oliver I. He eventually gave up the idea in 1656 because the Army let him understand that it was the one thing it would not stand for.

The popular forces organised in the Army had as their basic social objective a fundamental reform of the legal system, which would have had far-reaching consequences for the position of the gentry. Parliament voted to carry this reform, but Cromwell vetoed it. Then the Army vetoed the Kingship of Cromwell. And that was effectively the end of the matter. England was neither Monarchy, nor Republic, nor 'Constitutional Monarchy', but merely a military dictatorship. When Cromwell died, it floundered around for a year and a half before inviting the son of the executed King to come home and be King. No constitutional conditions were placed on Charles II. He was not required to acknowledge that his father had in any way exceeded his legitimate authority. And he was not even required to grant amnesty to those who, on the authority of Parliament, had executed his father.

Such was the fiasco of the English Republic. (I went into this aspect of English affairs in an Introduction to a reprint of *Good Work For A Good Magistrate* by the Rev. Hugh Peters, who was Cromwell's troubleshooter. Athol Books, 1992.)

The career of Lord Broghill (Roger Boyle), son of the Earl of Cork, shows what was required for effective loyalty during this period. He was a Royalist at the outset. After 1649, he became a commander of Cromwellian forces in Ireland. His success in that role led to his becoming one of Cromwell's close advisers at Whitehall. Then in 1659, along with another ardent Cromwellian militarist, Sir Charles Coote, he called a meeting of grandees in Dublin, which sent a message of loyalty to Charles jnr. in France, recognising him as Charles II. This enabled Broghill to be one of the great men of the Restoration.

The only way to be effectively loyal throughout those twenty years was to keep changing loyalties, and to have a sense of the moment at which it was advisable to commit treason against the loyalty of the immediate past, because treason was about to prosper and become the loyalty of the immediate future.

So what did it all amount to? Sir Charles Firth, a middle class Imperialist, sees it like this:

"...the rule of Puritanism was founded on shifting sands. So the Protector's institutions perished with him and his work ended in apparent failure. Yet he had achieved great things. Thanks to his sword absolute monarchy failed to take root in English soil. Thanks to his sword Great Britain emerged from the chaos of the civil war one strong state instead of three hostile communities" (*Oliver Cromwell*, 1900, p486).

The "absolute monarchy" argument is a figleaf concealing a non-issue, so that it need not be said that the whole affair was much ado about nothing. And Cromwell's achievement in holding the three kingdoms in one state only came about because Parliament had, in the first instance, engaged in wrecking activity.

But there are two more substantial aspects of the matter: what happened to Ireland as a direct consequence of the Puritan revolution, and the racial effect of Puritanism on English culture.

Mary Agnes Hickson remarks on the "confused state of parties in Kerry, owing to the constant intermarriages amongst the Irish and the Elizabethan or earlier colonists" (Vol. 1, p121).

When things began to pull apart in Ireland after the execution of Strafford and the movement against the Ulster Plantation, it was not immediately evident to everybody in Kerry which side he belonged to. For example, Dinneen gives the following letter to Ferriter from Lady Kerry, wife of the governor of the County:

"Directed: For my very loving friend, Mr. Pierce Ferriter, at Ferriter's towne in Kerry.

"These— * * *

"Honest Pierce, and I hope in God I shall never have reason to call you otherwise, this very day is one come out of Kerry unto mee yt by chance fell into the company of Florence McFiniene and the rest of that rebellious crew the very day that they robbed Haly who tells me that you promised (as he heard Florence say) to be with them the week followinge and to bring a piece of ordinance with you from the Dingel and join with them to take the castle of Traly, but I hope in God it is far from your thoughts for you that have ever been observed to stand upon your reputation in smaller matters I trust will not now be tainted with so fowle and offensive a crime to God and man nor give your adversaries that cause of rejoicing and just way for them to avenge themselves upon you nor us that are your friends that cause of discontent which would make us curse the day that ever we saw you.

"But I cannot believe any such thing of you and therefore will not take much pains to persuade you knowing that you want not wit and understanding enough to conceive and apprehend the danger and punishment justly due to such offenders; and therefore doubt not of God's mercie in giving you grace to avoid them which none can more earnestly wish an pray for than

Your loving friend, *Honor Kerry.*

Cork ye last of June, 1641.

"Here I am settled and do intend to stay until the times grow quieter which I hope in God will be ere long for here is news com of a mighty armie a preparing in England for to com over."

The "mighty armie" did not come for eight years. I do not know how Lord and Lady Kerry coped in the interim, or what form their loyalty took at various stages.

Entanglements between colonists and natives such as happened as a matter of course before the mid-17th century happened very little after that time.

After Cromwell, and apparently through the influence of Puritanism on general culture, a strong element of fastidious racist disdain becomes evident in English conduct. An American historian explains the racially clean, or genocidal, development of North America, as contrasted with the development of French, Spanish and Portuguese America, as following from the exclusiveness of Protestantism as compared with the universal human scope of Catholicism:

"Intermarriage between Whites and Indians was almost unknown... The antipathy of the English settlers to the Indians was far too great to lead to the sort of miscegenation which was encouraged by the French in their part of the continent... In the British colonies the half-breed was looked upon as an Indian, whereas in the French colonies, as generally in all colonial countries that had the Roman imperial tradition and the Roman Catholic religion, the half-breed was assimilated to the European group" (Madison Grant, *The Conquest Of A Continent*, Charles Scribner, New York, 1934 edn. p84).

Although the Cromwellian settlement of Ireland underwent some modification after 1660, and there was a further resettlement after 1690, it was in substance an enduring achievement of the Puritan Revolution, and was therefore sacred to the post-Puritan English state and remained without a historian for two hundred centuries. Its first historian was J.P. Prendergast, whose Irish ancestor came over with Strongbow.

Prendergast came across the realities of the Cromwellian settlement by accident. He was a barrister on the Leinster Circuit in the 1830s, and was apparently at home in West Britain, when he was asked by an English family that had left Ireland (Tipperary) in the 17th century to investigate their pedigree. (The relevant documents were not then generally available through the Public Record Office.) Prendergast was drawn ever deeper into the investigation and found that he was unearthing an atrocity. It was as if Hitler had won his war in Russia in 1941 and made a settlement with Britain (which would have happened as a matter of course in that event), and an inquisitive German of a later century, not doubting the "decent drapery of virtue" in which the state had dressed itself, had stumbled across the raw facts of the Nazi settlement of the Ukraine. The sense of outrage he felt caused him to write a full-scale book on the subject, *The Cromwellian Settlement Of Ireland* (1865). He wrote in the Preface:

"They [the Irish] were finally subdued in 1652, by Cromwell and the arms of the Commonwealth; and then took place a scene not witnessed in Europe since the conquest of Spain by the Vandals. Indeed, it is injustice to the Vandals to equal them with the English in 1650; for the Vandals came as strangers and conquerors in an age of force and barbarism, nor did they banish the people, though they seized and divided their lands by lot; but the English in 1650, were of the same nation as half of the chief families in Ireland, and had at that time had the island under their sway for five hundred years."

And in the Introduction:

"...it may be worth inquiring what were the crimes of the Irish to cause the English for so many ages to treat them as alien enemies, to refuse them the right to bring actions in the courts set up by the English in Ireland, and to adhere to their cherished schemes of depriving the nation of their lands. The Irish gave no national resistance to the English; they had no dynasty to set up; no common government to restore; no national capital to recover. They never contemplated independence or separation. The designs of extirpation were on the side of the English—the fears on the side of the Irish."

That is an entirely one-sided account. What the other side is I do not know. I have searched for it but never found it, and so I am left with the conclusion that there is as little to be said for the morality of the rule of Ireland for three hundred years by the English Reformation State as there is to be said for the three years of Nazi rule of the Ukraine.

*

When multi-faceted civil strife engulfed England and Scotland in 1641, it was inevitable that there should have been mayhem in Ireland too as a consequence. I explained some of the conflicting loyalties in Ireland, as they affected North Cork, in a talk given in Newmarket some years ago, *The Battles Of Knocknanoss And Knockbrack*. (This is included in *Spotlights On Irish History*, published by the Aubane Historical Society.) It also includes an account of the conflicts within the Confederation of Kilkenny, which made the Cromwellian conquest possible. I do not know what part Pierce Ferriter played in the affairs of the Confederation.

Note To Second Edition

Fr. Michael Manning, P.P., Millstreet, has made the following suggestion:

"I would like if there was some reference to the praise that the Nuncio, Archbishop Rinuccini, gives him in his *Commentarius* especially since he was a contemporary of Piaras. Also the fact that he was executed (15/10/1653) with his cousin, the Dominican, Thaddeus Moriarty, who is in the process for canonization. Rinuccini's commentary has been published but I don't know if it has been translated. I would love, if I had the time to visit libraries and delve into these sources but unfortunately I find that I haven't time for them or access to them here..."

The *Commentarius Rinuccinianus* has only been published in Latin, without an Index, and I have no Latin to search it. The *Nunziatura In Irlanda* was published in an English translation i 1873 as *The Embassy In Ireland*. The translator was Annie Hutton, Thomas Davis's fiance. The original was published in Florence in 1844, and Davis bequeathed to her the task of translating it when he was dying in 1845. Extensive notes which I made on it many years ago do not show any reference to Ferriter. Richard Belling's *History Of The Irish Confederation And The Wars In Ireland*, published by John T. Gilbert, with additional material, in seven volumes in 1882-1891, lists a Richard Ferriter as being taken prisoner at Knocknanoss, but doesn't mention Piers. Neither does the *Aphorismical Discovery Of Treasonable Faction*, written in defence of Owen Roe O'Neill by an officer in his Army and published by Gilbert in 1879 as *A Contemporary Account Of Affairs In Ireland From 1641 to 1652*. Ferriter is a remarkably elusive figure in the record of his time.

Available from the
AUBANE HISTORICAL SOCIETY,
Aubane,
Millstreet,
Co. Cork

*   Duhallow—Notes Towards A History, by B. Clifford

*   Three Poems By Ned Buckley And Sean Moylan

*   Ned Buckley's Poems (112 pages, paperback)

*   North Cork Miscellany

*   St. John's Well, by Mary O'Brien

*   The Yank By Tommy Power

*   Canon Sheehan: A Turbulent Priest, by B. Clifford

*   A North Cork Anthology, by Jack Lane and B. Clifford
        (176 pages, paperback)

*   Aubane: Notes On A Townland, by Jack Lane

*   250 Years Of The Butter Road, by Jack Lane

*   Spotlights On Irish History, by Brendan Clifford (172 pages)

*   The 'Cork Free Press' In The Context Of The Parnell Split:
        The Restructuring Of Ireland, 1890-1910 (172 pages)

*   Local evidence to the Devon Commission, by Jack Lane

*   Aubane School and its Roll Books, by Jack Lane

*   Aubane: Where In The World Is It? A Microcosm Of Irish
        History In A Cork Townland (200 pages)   Jack Lane

Aubane Society publications can also be ordered from booksellers,
or by mail order from our distributors:

Athol Books
P.O. Box 6589
London, N7 6SG

The 'Cork Free Press' In The Context Of The Parnell Split:
The Restructuring Of Ireland, 1890-1910

Redmond's Home Rule Party was overthrown electorally in Cork eight years before it was defeated in the rest of Ireland.

It lost eight of its nine Cork seats in the General Elections of 1910.

It was defeated by the All-For-Ireland League—a party which did not believe that John Redmond's strategy of gaining Home Rule through a tight alliance with the British Liberal Party, and in all-out antagonism with a Tory Party (or the Unionist Party as it then was), and with the Ulster Protestant community, could possibly succeed.

The All-For-Ireland League, anticipating the failure of Redmondism, tried to set nationalist Ireland on a different course of development. Its watchwords were Conciliation and Consent. It held that the important thing was to achieve a degree of unity within Ireland as a basis for a development towards independence.

But Redmondism held the line outside Co. Cork, and took the country to disaster.

After 1916 the All-For-Ireland League threw its influence behind the Sinn Fein movement for independence and helped to bring about the general overthrow of Redmondism.

The story of that remarkable development is told here, against the background of the Parnell Split, and the land purchase movement in which all-Ireland unity was achieved—a unity with political possibilities which were thrown away and trampled underfoot by Redmondism.

AUBANE HISTORICAL SOCIETY
1997
ISBN 0 9521081 6 0

Athol Books on World Wide Web

Further information about various magazines,
pamphlets and books, distributed by Athol Books,
can be obtained on the Internet.

Look up ATHOL INFORMATION at

www.athol-st.dircon.co.uk/